Chick Ink

40 STORIES OF TATTOOS—
AND THE WOMEN WHO WEAR THEM

Edited by
Karen L. Hudson

Adams Media
Avon, Massachusetts

Copyright © 2007, F+W Publications, Inc.
All rights reserved.
This book, or parts thereof, may not be reproduced in any
form without permission from the publisher; exceptions are
made for brief excerpts used in published reviews.
Illustrations by Matt Rhines.

Published by
Adams Media, an F+W Publications Company
57 Littlefield Street, Avon, MA 02322. U.S.A.
www.adamsmedia.com

ISBN 10: 1-59869-171-6
ISBN 13: 978-1-59869-171-9

Printed in the United States of America.

J I H G F E D C B A

Library of Congress Cataloging-in-Publication Data
is available from publisher.

This publication is designed to provide accurate and authoritative information with regard to the subject matter covered. It is sold with the understanding that the publisher is not engaged in rendering legal, accounting, or other professional advice. If legal advice or other expert assistance is required, the services of a competent professional person should be sought.

—From a *Declaration of Principles* jointly adopted by a Committee of the American Bar Association and a Committee of Publishers and Associations

Many of the designations used by manufacturers and sellers to distinguish their product are claimed as trademarks. Where those designations appear in this book and Adams Media was aware of a trademark claim, the designations have been printed with initial capital letters.

This book is available at quantity discounts for bulk purchases.
For information, please call 1-800-289-0963.

DEDICATION

Chick Ink is a source of strength for all women who face the challenge of being part of the so-called weaker sex. Those of us with tattoos, who voluntarily cast ourselves into an interrogative light full of misconceptions and suspicion, are slowly changing the misguided perceptions of the tattooed woman. To these courageous women, who stand proudly in their ink even in the face of discrimination and ostracism, we dedicate this book.

ACKNOWLEDGMENTS

This book would never have come to fruition if it had not been for the foresight of Brett Palana-Shanahan, who saw a need and provided a way to fill it. She proposed the idea of this book to the publishers, and then asked me to execute it. To me, it was like being handed a precious baby—a great honor to be trusted with something so special, but also a big responsibility, and it instilled in me a deep desire to meet and exceed expectations.

Reading all of the stories that were submitted for this anthology has been such a pleasure, and the more stories I read, the more I realized that this book was going to be extraordinary. For this, I thank every woman that submitted a story for *Chick Ink*—not just the ones whose stories are published here, but every woman who took the time to share her experiences as well.

I would not have been able to this without the guidance of my mentors, Barb Karg and Rick Sutherland. Rick, thanks for your great resourcefulness. Barb, thank you for spending so many hours on the phone with me, answering my silly questions, and just being there for moral support when I needed it.

To my family and friends, who understood my lack of communication for two months while working endlessly on this project, thank you. Special thanks goes to Karri Harbert, for brainstorming with me.

To my children—my beautiful daughters, Tessa and Ciera, who will no doubt be tattooed women one day—thank you for understanding why Mom had to work so hard on this. I love you!

Last but certainly not least, my husband and best friend, Don, who always has my back no matter how hard I lean on him. Thank you for everything you have done to support me and assist my efforts during this adventure. Without your backing and your willingness to tend to the many daily demands, a project of this magnitude would not be possible. You are my champion, and I love you.

CONTENTS

ix   **Foreword**   The Mystery of Tattoos

xiii   **Introduction**

1   **A Daughter's Defiance, a Woman's Decision**
     Shoshana Hebshi

7   **What's in a Name?**   Brandy Liên Worrall

13   **Rewarding Challenges**   Amanda Cancilla

17   **Beauty Isn't Just Skin Deep**   Ang Harris

23   **My Angel**   Amber Hallin

29   **Going Wild**   Arjean Spaite

35   **A Long Time Coming**   Rebecca Bandy

39   **Brothers in Arms**   Kathryn Godsiff

45   **Living Canvas**   Sasha Merritt

51   **Tattoos, Love, and Regret**   Alissa Nutting

57   **Shogyoumujou**   Andrea J. Morgan-Littrell

61   **Bye Bye, My Bluebird**   Heather Nellis

67   **My Mother, the Lion**   Alisa Gordaneer

73   **A Search for Balance**   Cathy Spencer

79   **The Innocence of Children**   Rachel Linda Ogden

83   **The Secret Tulip**   Joan Hobernicht

89   **They Don't Teach This in School**   Juleigh Howard-Hobson

95   **Living Large, Living Free**   Joanne Oliver Flanagan

101   **Smart Thinking**   Helen Kay Polaski

107   **The Turning Point**   Deana Lippens

113 **Happy Birthday to Me** Barbara Clark

119 **The Phoenix and the Pirate** Brett Palana-Shanahan

125 **Fish Out of Water** Annie Werner

131 **Armageddon and Elvis's Hips** Val Ladouceur

137 **Forever Eighteen** Catherine Lanser

141 **No Apologies** Kim Kane

145 **A Tale of Three Tattoos** Holly Janelle

149 **Moving Forward** Julia M. Shea

155 **First Impressions** Chris Marek

161 **Tattoo Fever** Tara Alton

167 **Grandma Led the Way** Michelle Swartz

173 **Beautiful Pain** Samantha June Engbers

179 **The Compass Rose** Lucie M. Winborne

185 **It's a Wonderful Life** Jean M. Miller

191 **A Small Price to Pay** Melody Barbosa

197 **Jie Mei** Liz Entman

203 **Pawprints on My Heart** Charlotte Brewster

209 **My Life as a Suit** Tara Goddard

215 **Just One of the Guys** Babette Lane Jinkins

221 **Future Tattooed Women of the World, Unite!**
Amy Brozio-Andrews

227 **Appendix: Frequently Asked Questions about Tattoos**

237 **Works Referenced**

242 **About the Editor**

FOREWORD

The Mystery of Tattoos

Tattoos can be strange and mysterious things, and I should know—I've been around them almost my whole life. Their designs and meanings are as varied as the people who get them. Tattoos can be a cross, a ribbon with a name, a beautiful blooming rose, a portrait of a lost lover, a child, a famous actor, a cartoon character or almost anything the mind can dream up. Tattoos can represent religion, commitment, remembrance, freedom, strength, and so much more. Some tattoos make a bold statement, some are for personal enjoyment, and some are for private contemplation. There is no one true meaning for a tattoo, there is no definitive right or wrong design. But there is always a story behind each tattoo.

Personally, I like being a tattooed woman. I get numerous compliments on my own tattoos, as well as the tattoos I do. I may not be a prominent figure in the world at large, but I'm well known in the tattoo community and on the convention circuit. Every year when I produce the "Marked for Life" international female tattoo artist convention I see more and more women involved in the field of tattooing, a dramatic change from when I began tattooing over twenty-five years ago. It's wonderful to see women finally take their place in the tattoo world, when they would have been ostracized for it just decades before. The tide is turning, attitudes are changing, and women are no longer outsiders in the tattoo community.

Being a tattoo artist may seem an unlikely career for a woman, but it's really an amazing job. As an artist I like to make sure when I tattoo a customer they are getting exactly what they want, because that tattoo I create will be a permanent part of their bodies from that moment forward. I listen to their stories and their reasons (or lack of) behind their tattoo choice and get to become, for a brief time, a part of their life journey. I get to share that life experience with each customer. Tattooing can be an amazing and rewarding occupation; my work will live on on that customer for as long as they live. It's a responsibility and an honor that not many other jobs offer.

In these pages you will be reading true stories about tattoos and the experiences surrounding the feminine aspect of tattoos. What's it like to be a female with a tattoo? What decisions drive women to get tattoos when there are still so many stereotypes against them? How does putting art on your skin affect your inner sense of self as a woman? *Chick Ink* is filled with stories of everyday working women, housewives, mothers, daughters, sisters—women just like you. Their common link is that they all have a tattoo story to tell. These women may have one tattoo, quite a few, or a complete body suit but they are all linked in the common bond of the feminine tattoo.

My hope is that reading the stories in *Chick Ink* will entice you to get tattooed—whether you are already tattooed or not— or will perhaps open up your mind to accepting tattoos and those who chose to wear them. And my advice: make sure you get exactly what you want to wear on your body; don't worry about the pain, if it hurts, it hurts only once; don't settle for less than you really want, and never worry about what other people may think about your tattoo. Tattoos are personal choices with personal meanings and personal stories behind them. Don't let what others may think stand in your way, take courage and inspiration from the women in this collection who took charge of their lives and made the decision to get the tattoos they always wanted. After all, if we don't give ourselves exactly what we want, who will?

Deana Marie Lippens *is the owner of Deana's Skin Art Studio and founder and producer of "Marked for Life," The International Female Tattoo Artist Convention.*

INTRODUCTION

Every tattoo has a story. It may not be an exciting story. It may not be the story you would expect. It may not even be a good story, as many of us have had to live with the regrets of tattoos we wish we didn't have. But the fact of the matter is, all tattoos have some kind of history. They speak the unspoken testament to the true heart of an introvert. They declare feelings of love, devotion, and sadness. Tattoos convey deeply entrenched emotions or just a simple appreciation for art.

Tattoo collectors, women in particular, face discrimination from those who do not understand our motivation for such permanent marks upon our bodies. They look at our tattoos and make judgments based on negative stereotypes that have been prevalent since the inception of body art in modern society.

Outsiders, who are only outsiders because they choose to be, see our art as primitive, barbaric, and unfeminine. Rather than looking at tattoos as art, they see them as mutilations and unladylike acts of rebellion. But what they fail to see is the true women underneath the ink. That is where *Chick Ink* comes in.

Chick Ink is an ambitious book with many objectives. To give tattooed women a forum to express themselves and to see that they are not alone in the world. To give the general public a chance to see past our ink and to hopefully realize that we are just like they are—the only difference is that we choose to decorate our bodies. *Chick Ink* also endeavors to provide a source of encouragement and inspiration to those who wish to become tattooed but haven't yet taken the plunge, maybe because they fear the social repercussions they know will be cast upon them.

Chick Ink may not change the world, but if it opens just one mind or changes one misconception, then it has made a step toward a better future for tattooed women everywhere.

A Daughter's Defiance, a Woman's Decision

SHOSHANA HEBSHI

My fingers twirled the locks of unruly hair, bound in a low ponytail. I stared out the window of my second-story apartment overlooking the gray urban landscape, which didn't quite encapsulate my dread.

I held the phone to my ear and grasped it tightly as I waited for just the right moment to tell her. I sat there, listening to her ramble on about the many wild songbirds in her native plant garden. Apparently, they show up to feed on seeds and sugar water. I was only half listening, my mind wandering. I tried to unscramble the words so they would come out right.

1

What I was about to say could very well alter the idealized Jewish mother-daughter relationship we had been building for two and a half decades.

"Mom," I blurted out during a pause in her monologue. I had tried to tell her earlier, when the ink was fresher. But now she was coming to visit and I didn't want her to find out the hard way—in the hot tub. I had to tell her.

"I have to tell you something."

I'd rehearsed this in my head. I'd rehearsed it out loud with my husband. I'd rehearsed it over the phone with my sister, who warned me that Mom would surely flip out.

"I got a tattoo."

Silence.

"Well, actually, I got two."

Here it comes. Stay strong. Don't let her break you.

I think I could actually hear her forehead wrinkling.

"Oh, I am so disappointed in you," she finally said, her voice strong but so far away. "That is so immature! And now you have ruined your beautiful skin."

I should have known.

She was always objecting. Objecting to me shaving my legs. Objecting to my getting pierced ears. Objecting to sun bleaching my hair. She even objected to me wearing makeup at a time when all my friends at school wore globs of sticky mascara, blue eyeliner, and frosted pink lip-gloss.

I guess I did know. I was to have remained her pristine youngest child until, what—marriage?

But she should have known too, I found myself thinking. I mean, I was the one of her three kids who was at least a little rebellious. I did take weight training instead of honors English. And I did wear the dangly earrings even after my mom forbade it, because it would stretch out the stupid holes she didn't want in my ears in the first place.

I knew it wasn't the religious taboo that made her so angry. It's more that tattoos are endemic of the dregs of society, and who wants a dreg for a daughter?

So I went into a rambling explanation of the rationale behind my two tattoos—one in the middle of my back, the other on the underside of my upper right arm—to deflect the guilt raining down on me.

"Kurt and I," I said, referring to my husband, "had thought this over for a long time before we decided on what to get. We wanted matching tattoos that meant something."

I described the artwork: a yin and yang split in the middle to fit in Japanese kanji characters that translate to "intuition" and "courage."

"This tattoo symbolizes the obstacles we've had to face and the theme of our relationship," I told her, trying to sound convincing and mature. "We've realized the importance of recognizing our intuition and then having the courage to act on it.

"The other is a Chinese character, which may or may not mean friendship. Kurt and I got the same thing on his birthday with his friend from college," I continued. "It's really small. You can barely see it." I left out the minor point that I was drunk when we got that one. Maybe I am a dreg.

"I knew it was only a matter of time, since Kurt has them already," she said. "He has so much influence on you."

Ah ha! She did know!

Wait. Did she really just say that? Well, maybe this will help assure her that it was, indeed, my decision, and I am not so easily swayed. "I'm thinking about getting a third—a *hamsa*—to mark my identity as a Jew and an Arab."

I thought that would win her over, or at least start a dialogue. My intention to permanently mark my body with this Middle Eastern symbol of this upside-down hand meant to protect the wearer from evil spirits was actually a memorial of my mother's maverick choice to create beauty and love out of a history of hatred. My *hamsa* would represent the truce my mother and my Saudi Arabian father made when they married and produced three compassionate, intelligent, and bicultural children. But, no dice.

"Well, I can't tell you what to do," she finally said. "But just don't let me see them."

Our conversation ended, and it felt like our relationship was forever tainted. That night I received a call from my ninety-year-old grandmother. I was surprised to hear her baritone voice on the other end and glad that she had remembered I existed. My grandmother is a docile woman. All anyone has seen her do in the last twenty-some-odd-years is sit at her dining-room table reading science fiction and mystery books, mail-ordering useless paraphernalia from catalogs, and donating money to political campaigns and organizations. I love my grandmother dearly, but I hadn't heard from her in probably a year. But when I heard what she had to say, my mood turned from delight to disbelief.

"You're not going to do anything stupid like this again," she told me. I'm pretty sure she was referring to the tattoo.

Who was this woman? When I had told her two years ago I was quitting my life as a newspaper reporter to run off with Kurt—who, at the time had pink hair, a pierced eyebrow, and no job to speak of—to the outer reaches of northern California, she seemed to take it in stride. This criticism over the tattoo

Famous *Inked Chicks*

Named after Shakespeare's love?
Lady Viola, born Ethel Martin Vangi, worked as a sideshow attraction in the late 1920s and early 1930s. She was referred to as "the most beautiful tattooed woman in the world," which could have referred to the beauty of her art as well as her body. Lady Viola's tattoos were stunningly intricate and her body was covered extensively. She worked the Thomas Joyland Circus until she was seventy-three.

seemed way out of character. She was supposed to be my silent, but powerful, ally.

So there I was. An exiled daughter—scorned, immature, defiled, and alone. Well, I did still have Kurt, though he might be a dreg, too.

I dutifully told her that I was done doing stupid things like getting tattoos. It was out of my system, I promised, while finding myself secretly wondering about an inconspicuous place to get that *hamsa*.

There's a passage in the Bible—Leviticus 19:29—that says: "You shall not make gashes in your flesh for the dead, or incise any marks on yourselves: I am the Lord." A rabbi's interpretation says that your body belongs to God, and you shall not defile it. I see it more like your body is a rental unit, and God is the property owner—so don't mess it up. What I'm not sure about is whether or not getting a tattoo is an evictable offense, or more likely just something that will eat up a little of my deposit when it's time to move on. What I do know is that while

I am living here, it is my home, and I want to feel comfortable in it.

In the aftermath of our conversation, my mom and I, more easily than I imagined, returned to our familiar roles. We have our moments when we argue or laugh or talk about deeply important world events or about what sort of spice would best liven up a piece of chicken. But we have never ever again discussed my tattoos. I seldom reveal the parts of my skin that are tattooed when she is around. When she does see them, I notice her eyes linger, and then look away in silent disapproval.

But I'm not about to apologize. I don't have any regrets regarding my tattoos. They are deeply personal and unique relics, which may change with time as my skin sags, stretches, and wrinkles. But their significance will never change. No matter what my mom says.

Shoshana Hebshi *is boldly defying her mother by moving 1,700 miles away from the California homestead to Des Moines, Iowa, where she will remain a freelance writer, editor, artist, an attentive mother to twin boys, and a wife to a struggling medical student.*

What's in a Name?

BRANDY LIÊN WORRALL

"If you was a boy, you'd be Marlboro," my father said in his Appalachian twang when I asked him why he named me Brandy. While this insight didn't appear to answer my question immediately, I began to see the twisted logic behind my father's penchant for narcotic substances serving as inspiration for naming offspring—and it made me glad that I turned out to be a girl. My parents also gave me my mother's name, Liên, which is Vietnamese for "lotus blossom," as my middle name. Because this was a name my mother had chosen for herself when she moved to Saigon to establish her identity as an independent woman (as opposed to her given name, Hai, which is a typical peasant name), Liên had special meaning and I was proud to carry it on.

Pregnant with my first child, I was desperately searching for ways to aptly name her without having her resent me for it. After all, a name is one of the most important markers on a person's identity. Like gender and appearance, a name is something most people are stuck with for the rest of their lives. I didn't want to be a source of torment for my child, and with a last name like Yu, there were all sorts of ways the name could go wrong—and the male Vietnamese name Phuc was out of the question.

Both my husband and I wanted something symbolic that would reflect all of our daughter's ethnicities and backgrounds. "Chloe" popped into my head one day and it was the first name I said that didn't make my husband cringe. Then there was the whole business with the last name. I wanted to keep my Pennsylvania Dutch last name in the family line, so we agreed that our kids would have the name Worrall precede my husband's last name, Yu. So, thus far, we had Chloe Worrall Yu.

My husband then explained to me that traditionally, the Chinese generational designator is part of one's name. His siblings maintained that tradition by including Dao, meaning "the way" in their daughters' names. Wanting to highlight my Vietnamese heritage as well, we decided that a Chinese-Vietnamese name was the way to go. Phuong, meaning "the phoenix," seemed appropriate, especially since my husband had seen our daughter's birth as a "rising from the ashes" after the loss of his grandmother just a year before. So we finally had it: Chloe Dao-Phuong Worrall Yu. Quite a mouthful.

"The way of the phoenix?" my mother- and father-in-law asked incredulously when we told them our decision. "Are you sure? Such an old-fashioned name!" My father-in-law then went into a long (very long) explanation behind historical and spiritual implications of the Dao-Phuong. When he was finished presenting the entire etymology of Dao-Phuong so that we were certain it was what we wanted to name our daughter, I smiled and said, "Well, it will make a very cool tattoo."

Everyone sitting around the table laughed nervously. I was joking, wasn't I? They weren't so sure.

And then it started—my mind went wild with designs of black ink, and I knew exactly where they would go. It would look great on my left shoulder blade with the tattoos I already had on my neck—the Chinese character for "rabbit" (the year in which I was born) and the crouching cat (the Vietnamese equivalent for rabbit in the astrological wheel), as well as the band of gold ladybugs (eight of them, the lucky number in Chinese culture) I had on my left arm. A simple phoenix, not too elaborate, with the Chinese characters for the name paired with the Romanized Vietnamese name would be the fate of my shoulder blade.

I looked at my husband and said, "No, seriously, it would make a really cool tattoo—don't you think?" My clean-cut, straight-laced, virgin-skinned history professor of a husband wisely didn't hesitate to agree, so I added, "And you'll get one, too, right? After all, she's your daughter. It would look funny if I was the only one who got the tattoo. We should get it together." His parents waited for his reaction.

"Uh, sure."

My father-in-law broke into a raucous laughter and said, "Tattoos! Good, good!" I appreciated his support, even though I knew my in-laws probably thought that this was more than a little weird.

Of course, I was advised not to get any ink until after I had the baby, for safety reasons. After I gave birth to our daughter, I wasn't really in the mood to get anything done to my appearance, much less a tattoo. When my daughter was only five months old, I became pregnant again with our first son. This time, the name came more easily. Mylo—because I wanted him to be mellow and the name sounded mellow to me. I kept saying the name in my head as I rubbed my tummy. We had already established a formula, so most of his name was set: Mylo Dao-something Worrall Yu. But what would the "something" be?

Even without the knowledge that the phoenix was traditionally paired with the dragon in Chinese and Vietnamese folklore, I thought "Long" would be a good name. It rolled off the tongue—Mylo Dao-Long. And yes, I immediately imagined that a dragon would be an awesome tattoo to have and even my husband had started to warm up to the idea more.

I was beginning to think that my father wasn't so crazy after all for wanting to name me after cigarettes and booze. How was that any different from wanting to name my kids for tattoos I wanted to get? How could I pass judgment on something that was imbued with meaning for him so much that he wanted to name me accordingly?

A few months before I gave birth to Mylo, my husband and I took an Alaskan cruise vacation. I woke up one morning and made my way to the dining area to enjoy a quiet breakfast by myself. Instead, I ended up being seated with a Republican family from Texas who were overly curious about this pregnant stranger with facial piercings and tattoos. They kept the conversation polite, asking me how far along I was and if I knew the gender of the baby. When they asked me if I had a name, I went into the explanation of the whole ethnic thing, the meaning, and how my daughter was named. They oohed and aahed over the complexity and symbolism until I told them that despite all of that, what my kids were really being named for were the tattoos I planned to get on my back. The maternal head of house seated next to me leaned in closely, touched my forearm, and whispered very loudly in her delightful Texan drawl, "Dear, I hope you know a good therapist for your children later on, because they're going to need one."

I thanked her for her considerate advice, the thick lines of the phoenix and the dragon inked in my mind's eye more deeply than ever before.

Brandy Liên Worrall is a writer and editor in Vancouver, British Columbia. Her poetry and nonfiction have been published in Amerasia Journal, *and she has published her Poem of the Day in a collection entitled* podBrandy one: first stabs *(Rabbit Fool Press, 2006). She is currently working on her memoir.*

Rewarding Challenges

AMANDA CANCILLA

When I was in college, striving to be a virologist with big plans to work for the CDC, my best friend started tattooing. I watched him go through the process of learning through apprenticeships and research. He grew as an artist, moved to Indianapolis, and began working in a highly respectable tattoo shop. I had always been captivated by tattoos, so I let him do a few pieces on me. As my interests steered from biology to art, I changed my college focus and pursued a degree in graphic design. But after a while, I began to have second thoughts about sitting in front of a computer all day, working on page layouts and business systems. While working on some freelance jewelry ads, I discovered that I had an incredibly steady hand. It was then that I decided to give tattooing a try. My friend helped me get started and I began looking for a job.

Almost immediately, I earned a job at one of the oldest tattoo shops in town. Admittedly, it was very intimidating walking into a shop filled with a very tattooed, very hard-core group of men. I was, and still am, the only female tattoo artist at the shop. I had very few tattoos myself and felt as if the other artists looked down on me for that. Clients would come in and think I was just a counter girl. Most of them were surprised to find out I was actually an artist. Some of them told me straight out that they would never let a girl tattoo them, and it would crush me. Over time, I developed a large clientele and a name for myself, so now I don't get that negative reaction as often.

I believe that the reality-based television shows about tattoos have also been helpful by featuring female tattoo artists. Many of my regular clients are women in their forties or older, and they realize that tattoos aren't what they used to be. Moms watch the tattoo shows with their kids and see that their peers are sitting under the needle just as often as their children.

There aren't many female tattoo artists in my town, and it has taken a while, but people are finally starting to respect the fact that we can be just as good as our male counterparts. There are, however, still stereotypes, which stem from being female. Most of the comments I get from coworkers and my industry peers aren't harmful. Most of it is just typical hazing that comes with working with a bunch of men. They joke that I get bigger tips because I have breasts and wonder (out loud) how I manage to tattoo without my boobs getting in the way. These kinds of jokes I can deal with—they aren't intended to upset me, but just to bring a laugh from the other guys. The hardest thing to cope with is the attitudes of my own parents and the general public outside of the shop.

My family is very liberal and generally very supportive. My father and brother both have degrees in art. My mom has more of a scientific mind. But both of my parents think I'm a little crazy and Mom doesn't like tattoos at all. "Make sure you cover those for so-and-so's wedding. They are not the kind of people that will respect your tattoos," she says, more to cover up the fact that she is mostly concerned about what they will think of her. I know that she comes from a different time when tattoos were more biker- and sailor-oriented, but she refuses to accept that things may have changed between then and now. I've told her about the clients I've had that are her age or older, particularly the eighty-one-year-old woman whose goal was to have a tattoo before she died. Mom thinks those people are as crazy as me. She's not vehemently opposed to tiny tattoos, but my Harry Potter half sleeve is a source of great disdain for her.

One of the most common questions I get from my mother and from random people on the street is what if I decide one day that I don't like the subject matter of my tattoos? What if I "grow up" and don't like Harry Potter anymore? I tell them honestly that I don't see that happening, but if it does, that tattoo will still represent a time in my life when it was very important to me. My half sleeve is a beautiful, award-winning piece of art that deserves to be displayed proudly.

My job makes me incredibly happy. The stress it creates from my family, however, is one part I could live without. In their eyes, I am a disappointment because I didn't attain the goals I set out with in college, and it hurts knowing that they feel I failed them. But all things considered, I am the happiest I have ever been in my life. When clients walk in with an idea and no idea how to translate it onto paper, I can do that for them. There's no feeling that compares to the smile that comes with the finished piece. I may not be changing the world, but I am changing the life of an individual forever. Whether it's a tribal armband or a portrait of a loved one who passed away, that tattoo means something to that person. I enjoy listening to the stories of the clients, their reasons for and thoughts behind their taking a step into a new life with a tattoo.

I would never change what I do. And despite all their joking around, my coworkers are really great. I intend to continue learning and collecting my own tattoos no matter what other people think. My husband and my friends are supportive of me and understand why I do what I do. It's about living a life that makes you want to get out of bed every day, a life that makes you feel proud to showcase your work, every chance you get, for the whole world to see. At least, that's what it's about for me.

Amanda Cancilla has been a tattoo artist at Artistic Skin Designs on the south side of Indianapolis, Indiana, for three years. She lives in Indianapolis with her husband, Jake, their four cats, one dog, and one snake.

Beauty Isn't Just Skin Deep

ANG HARRIS

Like everyone else, all of my tattoos have
stories, but my motivation for getting tattooed
in the first place and for my continued modi-
fications dates back to one particular day in my
life. I was twelve years old and I remember
that day vividly. My family and I had taken a
trip to the movies and then out for dinner at
a restaurant. Back then, they had a promotion
called "pay what you weigh" on the children's
menu. My parents, assuming that this would
be an economical decision, told me to get on
the scale. Although I was nervous, I complied,
only to discover (to my parents' annoyance
and my own mortification) that I weighed
182 pounds. I had always known that my

weight was an issue, but for some reason—possibly the humiliation of my weight being made public—I remember this as clearly being the defining moment that I was fat.

I didn't have a weight problem until I was about ten. Between twelve and twenty-two, my weight fluctuated between 181 and 235 pounds—pretty heavy for my five-foot-six frame. Like most young women, my weight made me very self-conscious about my body. Besides the blubber, I had stretch marks on my arms that I knew would never go away. I never risked exposing my body; I avoided tank tops and would wear a T-shirt over my bathing suit. I covered my body as much as possible with baggy men's clothing, concealing my femininity. I lost a lot of weight in college, but the self-consciousness about my body remained—until I got my first tattoo.

I had wanted a tattoo for as long as I could remember, but it had conflicted with my ambition to become an FBI agent and criminal profiler. That career encouraged me not to possess any "identifying marks." However, after a brief stint as a store detective, I realized that I didn't have the stomach for law enforcement after all. That afforded me the opportunity to pursue my other career option—academia. As a sociologist, not only can I modify my body as I please, but I have been given intellectual tools to analyze my own experiences of body modification and how they relate to larger social trends.

At the age of twenty-one, I got my first tattoo. I drove to Rhode Island with two of my friends, since tattoos were illegal in Massachusetts at the time. I had never been in a tattoo parlor before and wasn't quite sure what to expect. Immediately upon entering, I spotted a tribal dragon design on the wall and instantly fell in love. The artist gave me the price and my friend offered to pay for it if I got the tattoo. I agreed. After experiencing a great

Famous *Inked Chicks*

Maud Stevens Wagner was a high-wire performer at the World's Fair before meeting Gus Wagner, a tattoo artist with his own claim to fame, who continued to use the hand-poke method, even after the invention of the tattoo machine. Maud learned the art from Gus and began giving hand-poked tattoos as well, which became a family tradition they also passed down to their daughter, Lovetta. Maud is recognized for being the first prominent female tattoo artist in America.

amount of pain for two hours, my beautiful tattoo was finished. I was so proud of it, I went to a party afterward and showed off my bloody and inky bandages to many partygoers. This was the first time I ever showed off an area of my body with pride and excitement. I soon returned to the same shop for another tribal design, to cover up the stretch marks on my lower back. I kept my tattoos a secret from my family, but would show the ones on my back to anyone who would stop and look.

My first tattoos didn't have deep, significant meanings to me, but they provided me with a sense of pride in my body, which I never had before, and I got hooked. I began to get tattoos that were personally meaningful, like the Chinese symbol for "turtle" that I got on my ankle to remind me of my beloved pet. The pirate ship on my leg reminds me of *The Goonies,* which was one of my favorite movies as a child. The strange skeleton shape on my foot is a souvenir from my trip to Germany, and returns me to the small tattoo shop in Berlin each time I look at it. In this way, my tattoos gradually began to reveal aspects of my personality to others without me having to say a word.

Before I moved to New York City for graduate studies, I got a tattoo on my chest in memory of my grandmothers, who had both died within a year of each other. My mother's mother had died unexpectedly, but she had always wanted a tattoo of a rose on her chest. Since blue had been her favorite color, I got a blue rose for her. I never had the opportunity to know my father's mother, who suffered from Alzheimer's, but I had always admired her from the stories I'd been told of how, after the death of her husband, she raised ten children by herself in rural Nova Scotia. For her, I got the Chinese symbol for "strength." And for both grandmothers, I got the Chinese symbol for "grandmother." I feel that my most memorable tattoo is the piece I have on my right wrist of an angel coming out of the clouds and the Latin words for "from here strength and security." Above the angel's wings is a star with a circle around it, a depiction of a pendant on a necklace, which belonged to my great-grandmother, who used to call me an angel when I was little.

From that point, I got a dozen other tattoos and began to design the body I wanted. My tattoos have allowed me to think of my body as modeling clay or a canvas. Before I ever had any ink, I tried (unsuccessfully) to fit in with mainstream standards of beauty, but my tattoos have allowed me to reclaim and own my body, and define my own standards of beauty. In the eight years since I got my first tattoo, I have modified my body in many ways. I lost seventy pounds, began lifting weights, and got a breast reduction. I have over a dozen piercings, dozens of tattoos, dreadlocks, and I stretched my earlobes. Now, when I look in the mirror, I see a work of art, which I am enormously proud of.

It's interesting that I have transformed myself through a means which some would consider mutilation. It has helped me to reclaim myself and see beauty where I couldn't see it before. It does not define me, because there are many other attributes that describe who I am—black, female, lesbian, spiritual, and inked. Like the poet and theorist Audre Lorde, I feel the list that describes my various identities is endless. But without discovering body art, I wonder if I ever would have discovered myself.

Ang Harris was born and raised in Boston, Massachusetts. She moved to New York City five years ago to further her graduate studies in medical sociology and AIDS research. She currently lives with her girlfriend and her turtle in Harlem.

My Angel

AMBER HALLIN

It all started when I twenty-six weeks pregnant with my second child. My husband and I were walking around the mall and we came across one of those racks you flip through to see artwork. I came across a beautiful angel print by N. A. Noel called The Angel of Care, a portrait of a little girl angel carrying a baby up into the heavens. The waterworks came pouring out and my husband Marc laughed, chalking it up to pregnancy hormones, and we walked away. Just weeks later, we discovered that our son had a severe chromosome defect among other abnormalities. He was not going to survive. When we came home from the hospital with empty arms, Marc handed me a gift. I opened it and there was the framed artwork I had cried over in the mall a few weeks before. I looked at the picture, and to me that was our Patrick going up to the heavens with one of God's beautiful angels.

Permanent skin art was nothing new to me; I already had two tattoos. The first one I got was a gift from my husband after our daughter was born—a small tiger with a rose on my right ankle. My second one was a tiger (Do you sense a trend here?) with tribal graphics across my lower back. It was one year later that I decided to get a replica of *The Angel of Care* permanently emblazoned on my left shoulder. I went to a tattoo convention in my hometown and met a local artist there. He said he could do my tattoo for a great price. In the world of permanent ink, you definitely get what you pay for. It looked terrible. The tattooist had a hangover and made the image crooked. I went back to him three times to get it touched up and there was

Famous *Inked Chicks*

Ruth Marten is one of the first female tattoo artists to have a fine arts background. She studied at the School of the Museum of Fine Arts in Boston, Massachusetts, and felt that skin was the ultimate canvas. Her tattoo skills were self-taught, which may ultimately have been what caused her to branch out beyond normal tattoo boundaries. Ruth sought to bridge the gap between fine art and tattoo art, and became recognized for her art deco and nouveau styles, as well as highly graphic tribal art, offering her clients much more than the typical tattoo flash pictures.

still no improvement. While it healed, I kept praying that it would eventually start to look better, but it never did. What could I do? Unless I got it lasered off or covered up, I was stuck with it.

I decided I wanted it covered up. I knew it was going to cost a pretty penny, but I saw how people looked at it. And they would really look at it. It was so embarrassing. Even though they were nice and didn't offer criticism, I could tell what they were thinking. What was supposed to be a loving tribute to my son had turned into a horrible mess.

I started looking on the Internet for a spectacular portrait tattoo artist. This time I wanted it done right and was going to spare no expense. I searched tattoo shops within a three-state radius and soon discovered that I didn't have to look far from home at all. I found Megan Hoogland, owner of Cactus Tattoo in Mankato, Minnesota—only forty-five minutes from my house. I had never met a female tattoo artist before, and the thought really intrigued me.

From the moment I stepped in the door, I knew I was in the right place. I hadn't even met Megan yet, but I felt an instant bond with her as my eyes wandered around the shop. I realized that a female artist was exactly what I needed, considering my reason for needing this tattoo, since the last guy botched it and took my money.

When Megan approached me, I pleaded, "Can you fix this?" I am sure there was a measure of desperation in my voice.

"No," Megan replied.

My heart sank.

"But I can cover it up and redo it," she finished.

My eyes lit up and I saw the silver lining I'd been looking for. I decided to go for it. She was amazing. In what seemed like no time at all, I had a gorgeous tiger on my arm and my botched tattoo was gone forever.

On the outside, my tattoo was beautiful—it was everything I had hoped for and then some. On the inside, something was terribly wrong. I had covered up the tattoo I had gotten for my son. Financially, I couldn't get the angel tattoo inked right away. But I felt that I needed something to honor him while I was waiting to be able to get the angel tattoo. The only real, physical thing I had left of Patrick was his tiny footprints taken in the hospital. I asked Megan if she could tattoo them over my heart with Patrick's name and date. She did the actual size of his footprints, which are only about the size of a thumbprint.

Tears fell gently from my eyes the entire time. I cried, not because of the pain—it was the most pain-free tattoo I had ever gotten—but because of the intense spiritual experience. It looks like she took his feet right from the ink pads. Most people who see it don't believe that it is a real tattoo. Though it is my smallest tattoo, it allows me to keep Patrick alive forever in my heart and to share his story with others.

I was finally able to get my angel tattoo about six months after the footprints. I decided to get it on the outside of my left calf this time. I did that for a few reasons: the new angel tattoo is easily twice the size of the one I originally had done, which allowed Megan to add a lot more detail to it. I didn't have a whole lot of large, usable space left and I wanted to be able to show it off without too much difficulty, so my calf was the best location. Although it did hurt a bit, it turned out beautifully. I have gotten many wonderful compliments on it.

One day I was talking with my brother, who prefers black-and-gray tattoos, about my ink. "Well, I'm a sketchpad," he said, "and you're a coloring book." I replied, "No, I am not a coloring book anymore. I am a walking art gallery!"

I finally feel complete. Words can't express how elated I felt after the tattoos for Patrick were finally finished. I love hearing the whispered comments about my tattoos. Even more, I love it when people come up and ask me about them. It keeps my son's spirit alive. It also gives people a look into the more sensitive side of tattoos. I will never regret getting these tattoos, no matter what else I may go through in life, as they are so near and dear to my heart.

Amber Hallin is a twenty-six-year-old teacher at a day care center. She lives in Faribault, Minnesota, with her husband, Marc, their daughters, Taylor and Mckenna, their Saint Bernard, Thor, and cat, Zeus. Patrick's spirit remains with them always.

Going Wild

ARJEAN SPAITE

All my life I've had the curse of being the stereotypical "good" girl. I had done well in school, attended college, married, had three children, and stayed home to raise them through their preschool years. I'd served as president of the PTA and of the Junior Woman's League. I drove the kids to baseball and soccer practices and games, drilled them on spelling words and number facts, and did everything just the way I was supposed to. Everyone who knew me would have expected nothing less. I had never been the wild one.

I would never do anything as crazy as getting a tattoo.

Like most married women, I went through ups and downs, but for the most part I kept them to myself. I would share idle thoughts with my husband, but most of my friends would have been shocked to know some of the things I wanted to do. Even if I told them, they would have firmly pronounced that I wouldn't have the nerve to follow through on my wish list of wildness. They didn't know that deep inside me was a rebel just waiting to defend my cause. The first opportunity for this rebellious creature to appear occurred on my thirty-fifth birthday.

My husband Jim came home from work and informed me that he was taking me out for a birthday surprise. He wouldn't tell me where we were going—only that I didn't need to get all dolled up. We left the house, drove a few miles, and then he pulled up in front of a local tattoo shop. "For years you've told me you wanted to get a tattoo. Today is your chance. Either you get one tonight, or I never want to hear you mention it again."

Crap. I was cornered. It was either put up or shut up.

I hesitated. I was a PTA mom. I was back in college studying to be an accountant. CPAs couldn't have tattoos, could they? Especially female ones. I didn't know any women with tattoos. What would people think? But then, my inner rebel consumed me. I wanted to do it. So I took a deep breath and led my husband into the shop.

A mere hour later, I emerged from the studio, slightly sore but exhilarated. My right hip now sported a beautiful red rose—a rose fit for a wild-eyed rebel. Jim was impressed that I'd actually gone through with it, and I was thrilled at my uncharacteristic daring. I was my own James Dean.

Of course, by being careful to place it where it could not interfere with my career, I created a situation where most people would never know I even had it. Within a week, I was talking about getting a second one on my thigh, where I could still hide it when necessary but also show it off when I wanted to. Regardless, and despite my pride in announcing my daring act to friends, no one would believe I'd actually done it.

Things came to a head two weeks after my birthday, when Jim and I joined five other couples at a swanky restaurant to celebrate one couple's wedding anniversary. At some point during the evening, one of my friends asked what Jim gave me for my birthday. I replied that he given me two things in one gift—a rose, which would last forever, and a real pain in the ass.

All conversation immediately ceased.

So I told them all the tale of my hidden rose tattoo, but no one believed me. Fortified by several large, rum-laden, tropical umbrella drinks I suddenly stood up and in a very loud voice announced, "If you all don't believe me, I'll show you." And with a flourish, I dropped my pants—in the middle of the room—my rose beautifully exposed for all to admire.

Again there was stunned silence at our table—and all of the surrounding tables, for that matter—until somewhere in the background, a waiter dropped his tray. I don't know if our friends were more shocked that I'd gotten the tattoo or that I'd actually dropped my trousers. Either way, I was pleased.

By the end of that summer, I had returned to the same tattoo shop for my second glorious piece of body art. This time I opted for a butterfly on my left thigh. To me, it symbolized my newfound belief in myself. Like the caterpillar that emerges from its cocoon as a butterfly, so had I begun to emerge from the quiet shell I'd lived in for so many years. I was growing and changing, and I was proud of those changes.

Eventually, I even showed my boss my spectacular butterfly. I kept it covered most of the time at work, but I wasn't ashamed of it. Funny thing is, once my fluttery art made its way around the gossip mill, several other women in the office came forward to show me their own tattoos. Somehow, during the course of my rebellion, I'd become a trendsetter!

It was an entirely different matter when it came to my conservative father, however. He was still the one person around whom I was careful to keep my tattoos hidden. My mother had seen both my rose and my butterfly—and liked them—but as the youngest child and only daughter, I was still Daddy's little princess. I was sure he would never approve, and I didn't want to do anything to upset him.

For four years, I carefully monitored what I wore when I was around him, and he remained blissfully unaware that his daughter was now sporting ink. Then one day, I was attending a large picnic. My parents were there, as were my dad's boss and his wife, Rose. Knowing Dad would be there, I'd chosen to wear a long pair of shorts, which worked well to hide my butterfly as long as I was standing. What I had neglected to notice was that it showed when I sat down.

I was casually chatting with my mother and with Rose—Dad was nowhere in sight—when suddenly Rose exclaimed, "Arjean! Is that a real tattoo on your leg?" Before I could answer, my mother confirmed that it was, and that I also had another on my hip. We chatted about tattoos for a moment, and then the subject changed. Other picnic-goers had joined the conversation and I didn't notice that Rose had walked away.

She was headed straight for my dad and two brothers.

"Arnold, you never told me Arjean has a tattoo!"

My brother said afterward that my dad just glared at her. Without missing a beat, he walked over to me, bent down, and looked at my butterfly. I was horrified as I waited to hear his reaction. Princess was about to be dethroned.

For what seemed like an eternity, he looked at me; then he shook his head and walked away. My brother, who had followed him over to gauge his reaction, was disappointed. "I don't care how old we are now, if one of us boys came home with a tattoo, Dad would kill us! You get one and he just shakes his head and doesn't say a word." Score one for the princess and her butterfly!

Throughout the remainder of his life, Dad never mentioned it to me. My brothers think it's because I was spoiled. I choose to think that he saw the positive changes in my life and the symbolism of the butterfly. Though he'd never have admitted it, I think he actually liked it.

Today, I am proud of all of the things I have done in my life. The rebel in me—once unleashed—has never retreated. I think that when I celebrate my fiftieth birthday in a few years, I'll get a third tattoo. Perhaps a small dove, to symbolize how I am at peace with myself, my family, and my life.

Arjean Spaite is a freelance writer and editor. For the past decade, she has been a CPA. Spaite's writing honors include winning Friendship Among Women, *a statewide essay contest in Ohio. Her most recent endeavors appear in* Raging Gracefully *(Adams Media, Inc., 2006), and* Letters to My Teacher *(Adams Media, Inc., 2006). She resides in Boardman, Ohio, with her husband, three mostly grown sons, and a pair of pooches. She is currently at work on a novel and teen mystery series.*

A Long Time Coming

REBECCA BANDY

I developed a love for tattoos at a very young age. The first time I remember seeing a tattoo, I was about five years old, sitting on my dad's lap. He had an eagle on his arm, a leftover from his stint in the army. I asked him what it was and he laughed and said, "A mistake." But my interest was sparked and I've been fascinated with tattoos ever since.

As I grew older, I began to realize that tattoos were everywhere. My uncle had the name *Tish* inked on his forearm, which I'm sure irked my aunt seeing as her name was Glenda. I met a man who had an elaborate unicorn with his daughter's name in script underneath, and that really drew me in. It was the first tattoo I had ever seen that was customized and very well done. It really opened my eyes to the art and beauty of a tattoo, and I decided I wanted one for myself.

Not long after that, I decided I didn't want to just get a tattoo—I wanted to be a tattoo artist. I started drawing designs that I thought would make good tattoos, trying them out in marker or pen on my arms and legs. I was practically obsessed, stopping perfect strangers on the street because I noticed they had tattoos. I would drill them with all the usual questions— did it hurt, how long did it take, who did it, how much did it cost, why did they pick that particular design—I'm quite sure I scared a few of them.

The nineties arrived and tattoos started gaining a little more respect and popularity. I was overcome with the urge to get inked, but I was still too young. I found out my cousin had a tattoo, and then after his mother berated the artist for inking him when he was drunk, she also ended up getting one. I took a friend to get her first tattoo, and even took pictures while she got it done for her photo journal. I was wildly anticipating my eighteenth birthday and I had the whole day planned out—pick up a pack of cigarettes, register to vote, and get a tattoo.

But I didn't do it. When that day arrived, I realized I had no idea what I wanted to get. Tribal was a big deal at the time, but it felt trendy and not very meaningful. I didn't find any flash art that appealed to me and there just hadn't been any significant events in my life that I felt the need to commemorate for all eternity.

I met my husband soon afterward. He was tattooed and he found it amusing that I would be so obsessed with tattoos while, at the same time, still having virgin skin. "Just do it," he said. "You'll love it." But still, I waited. My sister met her future husband and not only was he inked, but his mother was a tattoo artist. I was surrounded by tattoos in every direction, and yet my skin remained bare and blank.

I had drawn hundreds of designs over the years, which I dismissed rather disgustedly—nothing was igniting my passion the way I thought that it should. I helped my husband pick out three more tattoos, and even designed one of them and watched it come to life on his skin. All of these things fueled my desire to do tattoos on other people, but I still wasn't ready to get one for myself.

My sister, after initially staring small with a koi on her neck, graduated to a much larger version of the fish, which went all the way from her knee to her hip. She also got a large tribal butterfly across her lower back. My brother-in-law got my niece's name in large letters across his back, and my sister's name across his neck—garnished with a ball and chain. They enjoyed reminding me how funny it was that they were all getting tattooed, but the girl who wanted to be a tattoo artist was the only one not getting any ink.

I picked the brains of everyone in every shop we went to—was it hard to learn, was it difficult to do, what do you use that for, why did you do that—fortunately they were all very accommodating to my incessant questions, but I still hesitated. I wanted one; I really did. But I wanted it to be original, beautiful, and perfect—and that is where I got stuck every time.

The pressure to pick out the first tattoo and have it be wonderful and meaningful at the same time made me feel like I was in some kind of headlock. My aunt came to visit and proudly showed off her latest art—horses, which she and the artist had customized to look like the ones she owned. During her visit, we went around looking at local tattoo shops together. It was her birthday and my husband was hoping to get her another tattoo as a gift. We talked about designs and ideas that we each liked, and at the end of the day—instead of my aunt getting a birthday tattoo—I finally got my first one. Just like that. And I'm thrilled with it.

I didn't get anything big or elaborate. I got my six-year-old son's name on my right shoulder, in his own handwriting. It's not beautiful—my son is in kindergarten and he's no John Hancock—and it's not perfect; but it is special and meaningful. And I love it, which is really the only thing that matters.

I'm glad I waited, took my time, and got a tattoo that I feel good about rather than something I got just to follow the crowd. I'm already thinking up ideas for my next one. Finally getting my tattoo has spurred me on to look into apprenticeships and actually fulfill my dream of becoming a tattoo artist.

Rebecca Bandy *is a tattoo enthusiast and aspiring tattoo artist. She lives with her husband and two young sons in Pennsylvania.*

Brothers in Arms

KATHRYN GODSIFF

Throughout their childhoods, our three sons asked for many things that we had to say no to.

"Can I go skydiving?"

"No."

"Would you buy me a motorbike?"

"No."

"Can we buy a farm with a golf course on it?"

"No."

But there was one question I had to say no to repeatedly, and it was asked most often by our youngest son, Tyrel—"Can I get a tattoo?" After being rejected numerous times, the boys finally stopped asking.

The next time the subject of tattoos was broached, Logan—the middle son—came home from high school with a story about one of his classmates. Apparently, the young man had returned from spring break with a large tattoo on his back.

"Really," I said. "I can't imagine his mother allowing him to do that."

"She didn't know," said Logan. "He got it done on the school trip to Costa Rica."

That revelation, relayed with a sense of awe at the daring of his peer, led me to an extensive lecture on the evils of tattoo, how it symbolizes rebellion, and the terrible risk of vile, blood-borne diseases from unsanitary needles in tattoo parlors, especially foreign ones. By the time the boys were ready to head out into the world on their own, my husband, Allan, and I were sure we'd gotten the message across. Putting pictures on skin was a ridiculous thing to do.

The bubble burst in 2004 when Logan, then nineteen, returned from a trip to New Zealand. It was his first taste of freedom and he savored every moment, traveling around the land of his birth with his best friend. He came home with a permanent souvenir of his trip—a tattoo of the Grim Reaper, in rat form, emblazoned on his forearm.

Prior to that moment, I'd never been emotionally close to anyone with a tattoo that could be seen by all. I was probably so prejudiced that a friendship would have come to a screeching halt with the first showing of any ink. I held tightly to my belief that people with tattoos must have subversive thoughts somewhere in their subconscious, even if it wasn't evident in their actions.

Realizing this, I struggled to understand the reason behind Logan's tattoo. He's not rebellious, is hard working, and has good morals. He couldn't really explain why he chose such an odd subject for his tattoo, but eventually I accepted the fact that he was just a fellow who wanted a picture on his arm. To my utter surprise, I was then able to look at it without getting that pursed-lips look, which mothers sometimes wear. Perhaps what I had thought about people with tattoos was wrong.

A year or so later, the boys—now all young men—decided they'd get matching tattoos. It would be over their hearts and read "Brothers in Arms." The simple fact that they'd all agreed on something was astonishing, since their youth had been spent with one or the other playing devil's advocate to the degree that they never reached a consensus on anything. Imagine a tattoo being a vehicle of cooperation.

Logan went first. By this time, he was an active-duty soldier in the army. Evan, the eldest—the one who usually faints at the sight of needles—went next. He didn't faint this time, and he even said it didn't hurt, much. And then Tyrel—who had asked most often for a tattoo—finally got his wish. I wonder if it was a letdown to actually be encouraged to get one.

Walking down a street one day, I reflected on how blessed I am to have such fine sons. They'd conquered sibling rivalry and were a united band of brothers. They were sons that any mother would be proud to introduce to her friends. And they had tattoos. I could hardly believe the direction of my thoughts—hoping someone would meet us at a pool or an area where the boys would be shirtless so my friends could see their tattoos—from a person who'd formerly judged people as unfit for knowing just because they sported a tattoo.

A thought popped into my head that I should let the world know how proud I was of my sons by getting—dare I say it?—my own tattoo. Now, that stopped me. While I didn't pass judgment anymore, and thought the boys' tattoos were great, I hadn't considered one of my own. I thought about it for a few

Famous Inked Chicks

The name Kari Barba draws instant respect and awe. Kari has been tattooing for twenty-six years and has won over 300 awards for her artistry. She initially started tattooing because her husband suggested it; she only agreed in order to support and please him, and they opened a shop together in 1983. Kari's son, Jeremiah, has also become a successful tattoo artist. Kari owns four shops in California, and works at the Anaheim location.

days, not mentioning my epiphany to anyone. In the end, I listened to my heart and declared, "I will get a tattoo on my ankle and it will read "Mother of Men." It felt better saying it aloud, as it seemed to seal my commitment and helped prepare me to share the news with my husband and sons.

I wanted to make sure they wouldn't squirm with embarrassment. I mean, an epiphany is one thing, but this was one that would affect our family forever. If they were really opposed, I wouldn't do it. But none of them made comments about midlife crises or acted as if it was too weird for a mother to do this.

While spending a weekend with Evan, I got my tattoo—in the same studio he'd gotten his. I knew he had high standards and wouldn't go anywhere dirty or seedy. The studio, named Holey Cow, was light and welcoming with black-and-white tiles on the floor. I was taken aback by the nice music playing in the background; I was sure there would be heavy metal blaring in my ears.

The shop walls, however, were covered with posters of dragons and strange imagery, which left me feeling a little uneasy.

I didn't want a dragon or anything weird; I wanted something pretty and feminine. And to be honest, I wasn't sure if the guy who would be my tattoo artist was capable of "feminine!" Much to my surprise and delight, he understood my vision perfectly and created exactly the kind of lettering I wanted.

I was sitting up on a table, preparing to get my tattoo, and that's when the nervousness set in. I already have a very low tolerance for pain and wasn't sure what to expect. I had brought a book along with me for some mindless distraction. Evan sat beside me on a stool, and was my pillar of strength during the entire process.

"It's like little bees, stinging my leg over and over again," I said through gritted teeth.

"You're doing fine, Mom. Breathe. It'll be over soon."

I closed my eyes and tried to focus on something pleasant. My tattoo. My eyes opened again and I tried to contort myself so I could see how it was going. "I can't see anything."

"Don't worry. It looks really cool. You'll get to see it in a few minutes."

It was surreal, sitting there discussing my tattoo with Evan. In my wildest dreams, I had never imagined this scenario. And yet there I was, standing in front of a mirror, looking at the finished product and feeling very content.

When we returned to Evan's house, one of his roommates greeted me with, "Well, where is it?" Turns out Evan had already told them about the "cool" thing his mom was going to do. I wonder if some of them told their mothers what Evan's mom did at age forty-six?

I'll admit to a moment's panic that night in my motel room. I had done something daring and permanent, slamming the door shut on the old mindset. As I looked at my fresh tattoo in the mirror, I wondered if my future grandchildren—and God-willing, great-grandchildren—would understand why I did it. I hope I grow to be the type of Granny who loves so completely and carries her pride in her family so obviously that her body art, even when wrinkled and faded, won't matter.

Kathryn Godsiff is a freelance writer, horse barn manager, and ex-rancher living in central Oregon. She whispers a prayer of thanks every time someone sees her tattoo and gazes back with understanding at what it stands for.

Living Canvas

SASHA MERRITT

As a painter, I have always loved the human form; its beautiful curves and variety of shapes. It felt like a natural progression to go from painting bodies to "painting" on them. But when I started tattooing, I soon realized that having a canvas that talks back and has opinions about its art is unique to the medium. The collaborative aspect of the tattoo process can be rewarding as well as challenging.

I had a unique experience during my apprenticing days, working primarily in tattoo shops owned and operated by women, and now, I own my own shop. So perhaps I've been a bit sheltered from the machismo of the business. I've been fortunate to have worked with some great people, and honestly don't have any horror stories to tell.

Tattooing people was initially frightening for me. I was terrified to make a mistake or do substandard work. Since then, I've gotten past the unhelpful fear—I had to or I never would have been able to do the work. I still have a healthy respect for permanently marking another person. It is a responsibility that I take very seriously. Once I had an artist make a mistake on one of my tattoos—I didn't even realize it until I took off the bandage. It was a terrible feeling, one that I continue to keep in the back of my mind as I tattoo others.

Causing other people pain was also difficult at first. I often inked too lightly, due to holding back, fearing I was going to hurt my client. But then I'd have to do it over again, prolonging the pain anyway. I am still sensitive to the pain of clients and offer them suggestions to cope with their discomfort, and I've never had anyone leave in the middle of a tattoo. I've also

Famous Inked Chicks

Mary Jane Haake initially learned traditional tattooing from long-time artist Bert Grimm, starting in 1978, and was Bert's last apprentice. While attending the Northwest College of Art, she did her thesis on tattooing, which was scorned by her professors. More recently, Mary is known for her influence in the cosmetic tattooing industry. She has developed her own line of pigments, teaches classes on the subject, and provides both traditional and cosmetic tattoos out of her Portland, Oregon, shop, Dermagraphics.

come to believe that pain is an acceptable part of the process—the cost you pay for permanently marking your body, a rite of passage.

As a new artist, I confess that I resisted inking the typical "girly" flowers and nature tattoos. I refused to become "the girl tattooist who does flowers." Fortunately, I got over myself; art from nature sparks my imagination and I love inking it. Now I can't resist the contradiction of "girly" flowers tattooed unapologetically in a sleeve or boldly climbing up a woman's back. One of my best clients is a woman with a half sleeve of morning glories, cherubs, and the names of her grandchildren; she also has flowers on her chest. Anyone who's ever had extensive tattoo work done, especially on your chest, knows just how fierce those pretty flowers really are.

I suppose I don't fit the stereotypical image of what a tattoo artist is supposed to look like. Aside from being female, I'm petite, not terribly "hip," and often my own tattoos aren't visible. One lady who came into the shop was startled by my appearance, because she expected the tattoo artist to be some big, gnarly dude. When she met me—well groomed and not scary at all—she actually giggled at her own misconception. Many people are surprised when they discover that I'm a tattoo artist.

Sometimes I'm not taken as seriously as a male artist might be. I've had men ask for, and then immediately discount, my advice or opinion. One man yelled at me because I insisted that his girlfriend speak for herself about what she wanted. One of my clients has gotten surprised responses from people when she tells them she was tattooed by a woman.

One of the changes I have noticed during my nine years in the tattoo business is the division of labor. Women used to work the front counter while the men in the back did all of the tat-tooing. Some shops are still like that today. Male-owned shops tend to have more centerfold-type imagery around, which isn't appealing to many female clients. The industry itself is still guilty of encouraging many of the stereotypes. I saw a tattoo convention once that was advertising a "best butt" contest, and I get persistent calls to the shop from companies trying to sell me pornographic movies. I've also had a number of men want-ing me to tattoo their genitals. I quickly learned the skill of the firm, professional refusal.

In the years that I have been tattooing, the number and diversity of the women getting tattooed has continued to rise. Most of my clients are women, and many of them specifically sought out a female artist. Their reasons vary from being more comfortable with a woman to looking for a more subtle style than what many male tattoo artists offer. I even had a male cli-ent tell me that he liked having a woman artist so if he winces, he won't feel like "less of a man."

As tattoos have become the norm among many younger women, they come to the tattoo studio with fewer negative preconceptions of what it means to get tattooed. I've tattooed female law and medical students, doctors, social workers, phys-ical therapists, writers, moms, grandmothers, and musicians—all of whom are changing the stereotypical fallacies, one brave woman at a time.

Many of my clients choose to symbolize significant life events with a tattoo. Art has always had the potential to be transform-ing by creating something beautiful from something tragic. It is very powerful for a woman to claim—or reclaim—her body. More women are coming to the art of tattooing to create works of beauty on or around mastectomy scarring. Memorializing the death of a loved one, particularly that of a child, has been a way for many women to take a step toward healing their emotional wounds.

I feel fortunate to be tattooing during an era when female tattoo artists are no longer considered to be unwelcome pariahs. I am grateful to all of the amazing women who paved the way and made it possible for me to focus more on the art and less on proving myself as "a girl who does tattoos."

Sasha Merritt *owns Dragonfly Ink Custom Tattoo studio in San Francisco, California. She has been featured in various art shows, including MUSE: Art of Women Tattoo Artists, the Virgin Art Show, Burn Out, and Fresh Meat. She also received an honorable mention in the National Liquitex Studio art competition.*

Tattoos, Love, and Regret

ALISSA NUTTING

My conservative mother refers to the time prior to my getting tattoos as "before she ruined her body." As far as tattoo culture standards go, at only ten tattoos I'm still practically naked, but to my mother I look like I just came from the jungles of Borneo. Each time I visit, she scans my body with a slightly constipated look, searching for evidence of any new drawings on my skin. When I told her of my initial decision to get my first tattoo, her shock was palpable. "The only people who have tattoos," she stated, "are prisoners and carnival workers." She then informed me that a man in her Bible study told her that I should be tested for Hepatitis C.

Although my family made me more than aware of the judgment those with tattoos can receive, it was when I moved to a right-wing town in Alabama that I truly became, I must admit, somewhat self-conscious about them. Recently while visiting at a professor's home, his wife came up to me unsolicited and gave me the name of a doctor who, she said, "can help you undo those mistakes."

Lately, this kind of social pressure has joined with my own change in perspective. One of the things that was so thrilling to my newly twenty-year-old self was the concept that tattoos are permanent. At the time, I couldn't imagine having anything for my whole life. I was drawn to the contradiction of it—in a span of time less than the average lunch break, I could have something that would last as long as I lived.

Clearly, people are drawn to tattoos for many different reasons. My husband, a tattoo apprentice who's been tattooing for over two years now, is a highly visual person and his tattoos reflect that. We make pilgrimages across the country so he can get inked by just the right artist for the job. To me, his tattoos are gorgeous but impersonal. If I ask him what his tattoos say about him, he'll shrug and reply, "I like good art." His priority is simply decorating his body in the most beautiful way possible.

I've used tattoos mainly as a way to solidify friendships and romantic relationships. My first tattoo, which I placed on my wrist because I figured there wasn't much point in getting a tattoo if no one could see it, is of a goat smoking a pipe. My boyfriend at the time had gotten a tattoo of its skeleton. My next tattoo was one of a librarian, in homage to books, one of my great loves. Then I got a handlebar mustache for my love of actor Sam Elliott (when I got that tattoo, the artist had to stop midway because he was laughing so hard). My best friend and I each got a flower made out of slices of pizza on our necks and the word *ukulele* underneath them, although that wasn't our original plan. We'd gone in to try to get guitars on our ring fingers in order to be "The Brides of Rock 'n' Roll!" (we had screamed this). But the artist informed us that he didn't tattoo hands. Our shock and disbelief took over an hour to fade, and we pestered the artist to explain why he wouldn't do them. "'Cause I've seen what it looks like after ten years, and it ain't pretty," he said. Of course, we couldn't wrap our heads around next week, never mind ten years. When we finally decided on the pizza flower and ukulele combo, I wasn't even sure what the correct spelling of ukulele was. "Go look at a dictionary," the artist pleaded, but we couldn't wait another moment. I realize now how lucky we are that I was right.

Not surprisingly, that kind of spontaneity led to some regrets. I got a large matching tattoo with someone I was dating roughly two weeks before realizing that it was not working out. Half of my arm is now devoted to someone who's no longer in my life. I took a big gamble getting a skull with my husband's name on it after we had been dating less than a month. I joked that if we ever broke up, I could just write "sucks" underneath his name. I guess I wanted to try to ensure what I was feeling at the moment would last forever. But, like hundreds of thousands before me, I overlooked the fact that if I wasn't happy in a relationship, I wasn't about to let a little ink keep me in it.

I was my husband's very first client—although victim might be the more appropriate word—offering up my skin as a practice canvas for him to learn on. I came away with three somewhat sizable, shaky tattoos, although only one of them is highly visible. While it's fun to point to my "practice" tattoos and

Famous *Inked Chicks*

Pat Sinatra has been tattooing since 1976 but was self-taught at the time. Pat kept a low profile until the late 1980s, after serving an apprenticeship under Carl "Shotsie" Gorman, who cofounded the Alliance of Professional Tattooists (APT). Since then, her business has flourished and she has become world-famous for her art. She's also a founding member of the APT and was the vice president from 1993 to 1995. Her shop, Pat's Tats, is located in Kingston, New York.

compare them to the professional work he's doing now, I have to confess that I broke the cardinal rule in "no regrets" popular tattoo culture; I wish many of mine were gone. The fact is, I got nearly all of my tattoos irresponsibly. I decided on some of the designs on the way to the tattoo shop and never asked myself if the meaning they held at the time would last.

Telling people I have regrets when they ask about certain tattoos makes me feel like I give a bad name to the many whose tattoos are mature decisions. Successful tattoos are products of forethought—knowing what you want, who you want it from, and what it means to you. Many tattooed people look down on those who wish their tattoos were gone, and I respect the logic behind their disdain. They feel that people, like myself, who have tattoos that they regret probably got them on a whim—a mere novelty—with no respect to the art. Yet the very thing that separates tattoos from other mediums of art is the fact that they become part of a living, breathing human. And being human, mistakes are often inevitable.

While my tattoos have not changed over time, what they represent to me has. I haven't gotten a new tattoo in several years, and I don't plan on getting any new ones without first giving them years of thought. My tattoos now stand not only as a reminder of fond (or not so fond) memories, but also as a reminder to slow down, think things through, and remember that there are consequences to our actions. Ironically, the very tattoos that some may consider "wild" have actually helped me to be more cautious about the choices I make in my life.

Alissa Nutting is an MFA candidate at the University of Alabama, Managing Editor of Black Warrior Review, and an assistant editor at Fairy Tale Review. Her fiction is recently published/forthcoming in Swink, Playgirl magazine, Ecotone, and Southeast Review.

Shogyoumujou

ANDREA J. MORGAN-LITTRELL

My life has been moving fast since the moment I was born. I'm a military brat and I learned at an early age that this world is fleeting. Moving every two years and scurrying all my life, I found myself longing for constancy, and it brought me a good deal of pain because I couldn't accept the fact that things in life are always changing. It wasn't until my adult years that I began to realize that the only way I might really have any happiness is by accepting that fact.

So when my friends started talking about getting tattoos, I thought to myself, *What would I want to put on my body forever?* I found myself drawn to the idea of transience. I'm in love with Japan and my degree is in

Japanese Studies, so I started thinking about getting *Shogyou-mujou*—the kanji characters that represent transience—done on my back. I mentioned this to my father, who had a meltdown and practically begged me not to get a tattoo. He didn't yell at all—quite the opposite—instead he sounded like a wounded child, pleading for me to listen to him. He made me promise I'd wait a few years before getting anything done, so I waited. I thought maybe I'd get it in Japan with my friends, but they wanted to get theirs sooner than that, so one of my friends got one that summer. She inspired me, but I wasn't ready.

While in Japan, my friend was looking to get a second tattoo and I thought I would tag along with her. I brought *Shogyoumu-jou* with me, four kanji that encompass the idea that the world is always changing and nothing has permanence. The studio had a foreign apprentice named John who spoke both English and Japanese fluently, and I was mesmerized. At first I was a bit apprehensive to have an apprentice maybe do work on me, but as I listened to him speak I began to respect him incredibly. I went back more than a few times and became good friends with the staff, but I was personally interested in the apprentice, so it was a motivating factor. I still hadn't actually gotten the tattoo, and soon I was to be leaving the country. I knew I had to do it now or I would be going home inkless.

I felt bad about breaking a promise to my father, but life passes us by! I chose the shop owner to do it, because I wanted it done by an authentic Japanese artist. Sensei is an amazing tattoo artist and he completed the piece in less than two hours, and that was with multiple cigarette breaks. It's absolutely stunning. They had a calligrapher artist draw the kanji to my specification. I wanted it stylized, but I wanted to be able to read it too. I hesitated about the size; it's rather large—about ten inches long and two inches wide. Sensei explained carefully that the integrity of the kanji would be lost if they were shrunken down, because over time with the aging of the skin, they would turn into little black blobs. So I had it done just as it was, and I don't have any regrets.

The pain wasn't horrible. It's a bit rough forcing yourself not to flinch, but I started laughing every time I did. I felt like Thumper from Bambi. It quickly passes and the beauty you're left with will last a lot longer, so it's worth it. I'm a firm believer in having friends do your artwork. Don't just go have "some guy" do it. Get to know your artist if you can. They're often great people who enjoy developing strong relationships with their customers, so try to get to know your artist while discussing what you want done. Tattoo artists who are true to their craft are incredibly hard working and take pride in what they do, so listen to them carefully and appreciate the experience of getting tattooed.

My tattoo is important to me because it captured an important phase of my life and it's about becoming the person I hope to be. I love Japan; I love the memories the people from that shop gave me. Even though it was painful, I forced myself to move on. Sometimes beautiful things happen to us and we want to cling to them, but we just can't because they're destined to pass and refusing to let go produces nothing but heartache. It's extremely hard for me to accept it when good things must end, but I want to be able to. I want to live my life accepting the good and the bad and knowing they'll pass in their own time. My tattoo serves as a permanent reminder and testament to those truths.

Shogyoumujou is a part of who I am now. I realize that my tattoo will only survive my body's existence on this plane, but as long as I'm living this life, I can touch my shoulder and remember that it's all fleeting.

I'll never forget the amazing times I had at that shop. It was truly inspirational seeing how dedicated the staff was to their art, and I'm really glad I had the opportunity to meet John. Tattoo apprentices work so hard to develop their skills. It takes years to master the art form; dedication and love is absolutely pivotal to getting most artists through those difficult years of training. I'll never fully understand all the work and effort that goes into becoming a tattoo artist, but I can truly admire and respect the men and women who choose to do so. I'd never trust anyone other than Sensei and John with my body, so when the times comes that I am ready for another tattoo, I won't mind flying halfway around the world to get it done.

Andrea *is a twenty-one-year-old college student, majoring in Japanese Studies. She fell in love with Japan because her Great Uncle, John B. Morgan, taught there at the end of the Meiji period and brought back hundreds of woodblock prints. This initial exposure to traditional Japanese art fueled the passion she holds for the Land of the Rising Sun today.*

Bye Bye, My Bluebird

HEATHER NELLIS

For as long as I can remember, I have wanted to get a tattoo. I toyed with a few possible designs, but then dismissed them as trivial or fleeting interests. When I was fourteen, I finally had a reason strong enough to get tattooed. My papa died of pancreatic cancer less than two weeks before I turned fifteen. I had been very close to him growing up. Although he was my mother's stepfather, I had never known my real grandfather, so he was extremely important to me. His death was the first tragedy of that magnitude I was ever forced to deal with, and it brought a great deal of emotional turmoil that, for the most part, was hidden from others. His funeral was not held until months later, causing even more heartache because I had yet to find any closure.

I knew that I would never find anything more important, or more worthy, of commemorating with a tattoo than the relationship I had with my grandfather. I was desperately seeking a way to mark the great times we had as a family, as well as the deep attachment I had felt toward him. I kept all of my pain inside, and I needed a way to express it outwardly. Shortly after his death, I began researching more and more about tattoos, the process, and the risks involved. I finally decided on a bluebird—a replica of the naval tattoo that sailors used to get after crossing the Atlantic. I chose this design because my grandfather was a sailor during the Second World War, and he was a bird lover; it was perfect. I put a lot of serious thought into the design and color of my tattoo, and when I was finally old enough to get it done, I went for it.

I went to a shop in my town—Toronto—called Way Cool Tattoos Uptown. I arrived with my drawing of exactly what I wanted, and I booked the appointment for the following evening. My mom came along with me for moral support. The artist who did my tattoo was Chris Hall, and I had a wonderful experience. He was very kind and gentle. I decided to have the bluebird placed just inside my left hipbone so that I could hide it easily when I needed or wanted to. Did it ever hurt! In the beginning, it hurt so much so that I briefly considered asking him to stop. But I just kept thinking about how badly I wanted it, and how much time I had put into it. Before long, it didn't even hurt that much anymore; I found that the irritating buzzing sound of the tattoo machine was much worse than the actual pain.

It only took about thirty minutes to apply the tattoo. Mom really encouraged and comforted me through the process. She even went back to Chris a couple of months later and got her own tattoo. My dad, on the other hand, was not too pleased. He made sure I knew exactly how he felt about it, but there really wasn't anything he could do to stop me.

When the tattoo was finished, I jumped up to look at it in the mirror. My mom told me afterward that when I got up, something was different about me; she couldn't quite say what, but the experience had really changed me. I was absolutely thrilled with my tattoo, and still am. Words cannot express how much I love the little bluebird on my tummy that will forever remind me of my grandfather and how much he meant to me.

Three months after getting my bluebird, I got a second tattoo. During my research, I read that it was advisable to wait a few years between tattoos, so that you do not get carried away, but I fell victim to a moment of spontaneity toward the end of Frosh Week. I had the tattoo done at Silverline Tattoos in Ottawa, Ontario, where I just completed my first year at Carleton University. This time, I decided to get a flower on the top of my right foot, and even though the tattoos were far apart on my body, I decided to go with colors that were similar to those in my first tattoo.

Although the flower did not have any significant meaning at the time, I did not regret having it done, although sometimes I wonder if I should have waited to go back to Toronto and have Chris do it. But I love it more and more everyday because I soon realized that it would not have the same meaning if it hadn't been done in Ottawa. It only took about twenty minutes to complete, and it was less painful than the tattoo on my stomach, but it was much more tender in the days following. I had to wear flip-flops for about two weeks. This tattoo serves as a reminder of the amazing time I had at university, the lifelong friendships I made, and all of the other incredible experiences I had. Every time I look at this tattoo, it brings a huge smile to my face.

I have had mixed reactions to my tattoos from other people. Some think that I must be a wild child—crazy and out of control—which is definitely not the case. Though I can be somewhat of a renegade, with a strong distaste for authority, my tattoos were not acts of rebellion in any sense. It was just something that I had always been interested in doing, an artistic act that satisfied my need for self-expression. Many people are quite taken aback at the sight of a conservative-looking, young girl (I am only nineteen), with two tattoos! For the most part, though, their reactions are positive because the colors and designs of my tattoos are both very feminine and bright—not what most people would expect a tattoo to be.

My friends really like my tattoos, and I think my experiences have encouraged them to consider getting tattooed. Although my mom and I were not tattooed at the same time, nor do we have matching tattoos, I feel like it was an incredible bonding experience for us. She has always been my best friend, and we were both there to support each other when we got our first tattoos. My mom is thirty years older than me; I got my first tattoo when I was eighteen, she got hers when she was forty-eight. It just goes to show you that tattooing is an art that is reaching women of all ages and from all different walks of life.

My father has yet to warm up to them, but I have learned that some people just do not understand the need that some people have to be tattooed. He says that every time he sees his little girl's tattoos, it hurts him like only a father could be hurt. I just respond to him by saying, "How can it hurt you to see your daughter this happy and confident with herself?" He is worried that my tattoos will prevent me from being taken seriously and being employed in the future, but I am not concerned in the least. I can easily cover up both of my tattoos, and I wouldn't want to work in such an oppressive environment that tattoos are looked upon with disdain anyway. Besides, in the future, those without tattoos will be the minority in the world.

Before I got my first tattoo, I was quite confident I would only want one, despite hearing countless people describing how addictive tattooing can be. I soon discovered that they were right; I was planning out my second tattoo on the car ride home from getting the first one, and I have already thought about getting a third tattoo. I'm not sure what I will get, but I will without a doubt get another one someday, maybe even a fourth. I've got plenty of time and a lot of blank skin left to work with.

Heather Nellis just completed her first year at Carleton University in Ottawa, Ontario. Heather has a passion for languages. Her major is French, and she has also studied Spanish and sign language, and hopes to learn Italian next. Her ambition is to work as a translator, interpreter, or a writer when she graduates.

My Mother, the Lion

ALISA GORDANEER

When I was twenty-five, my mother made me
get a tattoo.

Well, it wasn't as if she actually marched
me into the nearest tattoo parlor to mark
some obscure rite of quarter-century passage.
Rather, she cajoled me. "Come on," she
said. "I'm not going in there alone."

It started out as a joke. It was the early
nineties, and it seemed like everyone was
getting tattoos. Even my otherwise conservative boyfriend had recently gotten a small
constellation of Orion inked onto his shoulder blades. I'd trace its outline at night, con-
necting the dots.

One Sunday dinner not long afterward,
he was talking about his ordeal. He said it

hurt, but not that badly, really. That conversation turned into one about the number of people we knew who had tattoos. They were all men, as far I could recall.

"I don't want one," I said. "I couldn't imagine what kind of picture I'd like well enough to have with me permanently."

"I figure the stars are with us permanently," my boyfriend stated, rather defensively.

"Well, I want one," my mother announced.

"You?" I couldn't believe what I was hearing.

"Yes. Me."

"What would you get? A flower? The FTD Mercury guy?" I joked, teasing her about her business as a florist. "Or would you get Dad to design something for you?"

"Leave me out of this," my dad chimed in. "I'm an artist, not a miracle worker."

My mother looked serious. "I'd get a Finnish lion." She'd obviously given this some thought.

"How is that different from a just-started lion?" I teased, still not believing she meant it.

"The one on Finland's Coat of Arms," she explained. It's a rampant lion standing on a curved sword, with a sword in one of its paws."

I imagined my mother with a huge crest on her arm, and tried not to laugh. But my boyfriend leaned forward in his chair, clearly intrigued. "Where would you put it?" he asked.

"I don't know yet. Maybe on my hip. Somewhere it's not going to show when I'm at work."

"If it's not going to show, then what's the point?" I asked.

"It only shows when you want it to," my boyfriend pointed out. "That's why mine's on my back."

"You can't even see yours without a mirror."

My mother shook her head, indicating that I just didn't get it. "That's not the point."

"I didn't know your mom is so cool," my boyfriend said on our way home.

"She'll never really do it," I scoffed. "She's fifty-five. That's the age when people are supposed to be thinking about de-wrinkling themselves, not inking themselves."

"I think she should," he said. "Why not?"

But the matter didn't come up again, at least not for a few months—until it was getting close to Christmas, and my boyfriend and I were trying to think of the perfect gift for my mom, the perpetually impossible-to-buy-for woman. A scarf? Nah. Books? No, she just borrows mine. Kitchen gizmos? Forget it; she'd disown us all. I usually resorted to joke gifts—a Davy Crockett hat with eyes on it one year, and a box of popcorn another. What could top those?

"How about a tattoo?" I joked. "She said she wanted one, remember?"

My boyfriend's eyes lit up. "Great idea! I'll go down and get her a gift certificate tomorrow."

But the people at the tattoo shop couldn't tell him what amount the gift certificate should be until they knew what image we had in mind. I set out to find a picture of the coat of arms she'd mentioned—which meant, in the days before the Internet, spending hours on end in the library, combing through books of Finnish history and politics until I finally found a line drawing of the lion she'd told us about. I learned that the lion had been a Finnish symbol since the 1500s, and the two swords were the symbols of Karelia, the part of Finland where my mother was born, which my grandfather had gone to war to defend against Russia. The lion was a symbol of stubborn strength, which described my mom perfectly. It made a lot more sense now. I tried to imagine the lion etched somewhere on my mother's skin as I photocopied it to take home.

"We can't just hand her an envelope," I said, when my boyfriend came home with the gift certificate from the tattoo shop. "She'll guess."

So we tucked the envelope inside the folded photocopy of the lion, and put the whole thing in a small box inside a larger cardboard box. As I wrapped it in festive paper, I giggled at the prospects of her reaction.

Utter disbelief, it turned out, was her response. She had unwrapped the bigger box, then the smaller one, then looked quizzically at the photocopied image. And then she peeked inside the envelope. "You shits!" she shrieked, after a moment of stunned silence. "Now I have to actually do it!" We grinned, satisfied that we'd pulled off the most clever Christmas gift yet.

But she didn't rush down to the tattoo shop as soon as the holidays were over. In fact, months went by and she didn't go. "What's taking you so long to get around to it?" I asked.

"I'll get there. But I want you to come with me."

"Fine," I said. "But I'm just going for support. I'm not getting a tattoo."

It was around that time that I had my wisdom teeth removed—a tremendous ordeal, especially since I harbored a severe phobia of dentists and needles. But I lived through it, and I was able to admit to myself that my fear of needles was another reason I could never get a tattoo. And yet, I'd lived through that. I started to think more about tattoos, and I allowed myself to wonder what I would get if I were ever so daring.

I knew I didn't want someone else's art on me, no matter how historically significant it may be. I didn't want anything tribal, because my heritage was more Finnish than anything, and I'd discovered that the most tribal crest of the Finns was that of Lapland, which depicted a wild man in a loincloth. No thanks.

I started to doodle ideas in my notebook, trying to come up with something that was personally significant, tasteful, and small enough to be within my budget. Besides, there were still needles involved, and I still didn't really want a tattoo. But I wanted to be prepared—just in case.

"She's got to use that gift certificate soon," my boyfriend said. "It's going to expire and it will have been a total waste of money." So I reminded her. And reminded her again.

Finally, one September day, she decided it was time. "That gift certificate only has a few more months before it expires," she announced. "Let's go this afternoon."

"I'll hold your hand, but I don't want to get a tattoo," I repeated.

But when we got to the tattoo place and approached the door, she stopped dead. "I'm only going to get it done if you get one, too," she said firmly.

I had anticipated this moment. I had my notebook, with the design I liked, in my backpack. "If I can do it, so can you," she said. Slowly, I nodded, and in we went.

It took less than fifteen minutes to ink the small black spiral shell shape onto my ankle. It was somewhat visible, but not obtrusive, and it was my own design. The cute guy who held the buzzing needle smiled and stopped whenever the pain got too intense, which was quite often. But overall, I told him, it wasn't as bad as having my wisdom teeth out.

I admired my new ink, thinking how I would now always know I was me, and waited for my mom to get done with hers. Since it was a larger and more intricate piece, it was taking a lot longer. She grimaced at me when I went in to watch.

"Look what you've got me into!" she said, half laughing, half crying.

"Look what you've got me into!" I said, distracting her with an acrobatic move as I lifted my leg to show her.

"That's nice," she said.

"So's yours," I replied, watching as the tattoo artist buzzed the lion's mane onto her belly, just to the left of the C-section scar from which I'd been born.

Alisa Gordaneer lives and writes on an urban homestead in Victoria, British Columbia, with her husband and two small children. She is the editor of Monday Magazine, *Victoria's alternative newsweekly. Her work has been published extensively, and she has won several awards for her poetry and journalism.*

A Search for Balance

CATHY SPENCER

*"Art is a shadow of what a person is thinking . . .
a small glimpse of what they hold inside. Little secrets,
regrets, joys . . . every line has its own meaning"*
—Sarah,
Los Cerros Middle School, 1999

Every tattoo also has its own meaning. My
tattoo artist, Jim, tells me that I am into that
"cryptic stuff," and I suppose he's right. All of
my tattoos have some kind of deep personal
significance. Others may not understand
them, but they don't have to. My art is for me
and no one else.

I got my first tattoo thirteen years ago.
I had been interested in tattoos for some

time and knew that I wanted one. I knew where I wanted it long before I knew what it would look like. I would have it done on my shoulder, so it could be easily covered up and out of sight, yet in an area that I could show off without getting undressed. The need to have the ability to cover it was driven by the fact that I was searching for a teaching job. I was concerned that the still-prevalent social stigma of tattoos, especially toward women with them, could affect my ability to get a job.

Once I had decided on the "where," figuring out the "what" took a little longer. After much deliberation, I decided that I wanted a man in the moon to symbolize the fact that I always have family and friends looking out for me. I wanted to have the moon coming through the clouds to remind me that, even when there is darkness, there is also light—the proverbial silver lining behind every dark cloud.

I wanted two stars to represent two of the most difficult times in my life. I wanted to remember what I had been through, because those challenges and struggles were part of what made me who I am today.

Finally, I would get a shooting star to encourage me to continue dreaming, and to strive to attain those dreams.

Those images are all a part of my tattoo now. To look at it, you wouldn't realize that it represents chapters in my life. But it does, and it is because of that deep spiritual connection that I have never once regretted my tattoo.

Thirteen years later, my first tattoo started to make even more sense than I realized it would. I was diagnosed with cyclothymia, a form of depression similar to bipolar disorder, but in a milder form. From the information that I shared with my doctor, it was determined that I had actually struggled with this disorder all of my life. The ups and downs of my disorder were all there in my tattoo all along. I derived even more strength and comfort from my tattoo as I faced my illness.

With the help of medication and therapy, I began to feel better, and decided I wanted another tattoo. I wasn't sure what to get again, so periodically I would think about it and search for ideas on the Internet. One day, as I was perusing through Asian characters for balance, I came upon the yin-yang symbol. I did more searching and found an image by Zachary Miller that contained a Zen circle, yin-yang, Heyiya-if, and Mu. I researched these symbols and learned about them, not only from Zachary's Web site, but other resources as well.

I learned that the yin-yang is a famous symbol of Taoism and it represents balance between opposing forces. The nature of my disorder is struggle—the struggle between the highs and the lows. Next, I learned about the Heyiya-if, or never-ending spiral. Similar to the yin-yang, it has the two arms of a spiral

Famous Inked Chicks

Rusty Skuse got her first tattoo in 1961 from her future husband, tattoo artist Bill Skuse. Her first tattoo was the result of a dare, but she continued collecting from that point. By the time she was twenty, she had sixty-two tattoos and gained media attention when the British army (in which she served as a private) required her to keep all of them covered when in uniform, although male soldiers were not bound by this same rule. In 1970, Rusty won Guinness Record status as Britain's most tattooed lady, a position that she still holds today.

growing ever closer but never touching—representing life and death, earth and sky, concrete and spiritual—with the center as the magical transition between the pairs. Again, this mirrored my disorder and how it makes me feel.

The Zen circle is a single, quickly brushed stroke made by the human hand. Although there is no starting or ending point, the beginning and end are clearly defined. The circle itself represents the path of life from birth to death. Mu, a character from a Japanese tea ceremony scroll that means the "nothingness of the universe," I decided not to include that element in my tattoo.

I thought about where I wanted my art and I knew it had to be somewhere that I could see it. I determined that my wrist would be the perfect placement. As I talked with my husband about it, he got involved in drawing up my idea. I showed friends to see what they thought. I contemplated my color choices and decided that green and black would represent life and death, while blue would create balance, which again cryptically symbolized my own personal struggles.

Needless to say, I sought out Jim again and had him begin working on drawing my tattoo. It took a few visits until I was comfortable with the results, but Jim came through with exactly what I was looking for. After changing my mind a few times, my tattoo went from a two-dimensional image on my wrist to a three-dimensional tattoo on my ankle. It was Jim's idea to turn the yin-yang on its side with a three-dimensional view. He never stopped working on or thinking about my tattoo. Now I have a gorgeous band around my ankle that represents the daily struggles I endure.

Jim and I are now working on more cryptic symbols to add on to my first tattoo. We are in the process of incorporating the planet Saturn with two moons, symbols for my marriage and two sons—positive symbols to balance out the tragic ones already represented with the two stars.

My tattoos have been a strong, influential force in my life. I find the process—from start to finish—to be empowering and even relaxing. I tease Jim that I'm going to visit the shop just to hang out on the couch and unwind to the soothing sounds of the tattoo machine, buzzing and inking away. I'm actually working on making a recording of the machine buzzing so I can enjoy the sound away from the shop when I'm feeling anxious. It really has a calming effect on me, like a white noise.

Not only have my tattoo experiences been positive and fulfilling, they have been therapeutic. I will never regret them, as they have taught me to look forward, not back.

Cathy Spencer is a thirty-five-year-old special education teacher in Pennsylvania. She lives with her husband, Ron, and their two sons, Shayne and Dylanger. Her tattoo artist, Jim, works at New Image Tattoo in Bernville. The artwork by Zachary Miller can be found at http://zach.chambana.net/gallery/zarf/tat.html.

The Innocence of Children

RACHEL LINDA OGDEN

According to other people, I do not look like the type of person who would have one tattoo, let alone ten. And yet, when someone says that, I don't think they even realize that they are stereotyping people with tattoos. It comes across as such an innocent statement—"Wow, you have a tattoo! You look so sweet and innocent." I've heard it so many times, but I hope I am breaking their stereotypical views by showing them that people with tattoos don't deserve to be pigeonholed in a separate, single category.

Of course, being a girl with tattoos just adds to the stigma. Many of my tattoos are visible, and there is no realistic way for me to hide them. Not that I'd want to anyway;

I love my ink. I'll admit that there are a few jobs I probably didn't get because of them, but I'm still in school. I'm working to become an elementary special education teacher and apparently there is more flexibility allowed for appearance in that field. The school where I plan to teach is all special education, and the teaching approach is very nontraditional, so I believe I will fit in just fine.

There have been a few occasions where I had to do observations in the classroom setting, and the kids loved my tattoos. One sweet, little girl in particular was fascinated by a butterfly tattoo that I have on my wrist. It is probably the worst tattoo I own. It was done on an impulse at a shop that I don't plan to ever return to. It had to be touched up and then completely redone at a different shop. But to this little girl, it was a beautiful butterfly that I had sitting on my wrist and it stayed there all the time. Eventually, some of the other kids began to look and I was really surprised by their reactions. They're so pure and nonjudgmental. Unfortunately, those qualities tend to fade away as we grow older.

I have gotten "the look" a few times when people saw my tattoos, especially if I was wearing a sleeveless shirt, which makes the big tattoo on my arm very visible. Some people seem to find this an odd place for a girl to have a tattoo—even some other girls who have a few tattoos themselves.

I used to have a very nice Celtic symbol on my arm, and then I got the bright idea to have it removed via laser treatments. I thought the tattoo would just disappear after a few sessions, but instead I ended up with an ugly, bumpy scar and essentially threw my money away. I lived with the scar like that for about two years and then I got a tattoo over it. Fortunately, the process of getting tattooed over the scarring helped diminish some of the roughness. Considering how bad the scarring was in the beginning, it turned out quite well. To cover it up most effectively, the artist had to use a lot of black in the tattoo, so it ended up being a tribalesque design with roses in it to give it a feminine touch. As a result of this whole horrifying ordeal, I am much more careful about what I get, where I'm getting it, and who the artist will be.

All of my tattoos have some type of meaning to me, even if I did get a few of them on impulse. I have the Chinese symbols for husband and wife on my ring fingers to represent my marriage. Even though they are the smallest and simplest of all of my tattoos, they have the most meaning to me. My sister and I also have the Chinese symbol for friendship on the insides of our wrists. A lot of times, sisters don't get along or they lead separate lives, never developing a strong bond. We decided to get the symbol for friendship because we get along so well and always do things together.

Some of my tattoos are simply of things I love, like flowers, the sun, the moon, and stars. The world around us is here for our enjoyment and I'm really starting to appreciate the little things more than I used to. For example, when you add a vase of fresh flowers to a room, it transforms the mood of the room. When I see the flowers around my wrist, it makes me feel cheerful, just as flowers send cheer to those we give them to.

I plan on getting more tattoos in the future. Once I am done with school and have paid off my student loans, I want to get a back piece. I already know I am going to have to carefully plan out this one. It is such a big area and the possibilities are just about endless on what you can do there. I also plan to get some kind of symbolic tattoo to represent my two kids and one for my dogs. Without my kids, my life would not have gotten put on the right path.

My tattoos are an integral part of me and sometimes, when I least expect it, someone will compliment one of them. When my daughter was born, I had to have a C-section. During the delivery prep, as I was getting my epidural, the nurses were asking me about my tattoos and they seemed to like them. That really helped me get my mind off the situation, and I—like most people—enjoy talking about my ink. One of the nurses there also had a tattoo, and she shared her story as well. Then some of the other nurses started talking about the tattoos they'd like to get. My daughter, who is now five, already wants a tattoo. I wonder if hearing all of that tattoo talk has anything to do with it.

Rachel Ogden has been married for nine years and has two children. She decided to go back to school for early childhood education and hopes to graduate within the next year and a half. Having kids and going to school has been challenging, but she knows the rewards will surpass the difficulties.

The Secret Tulip

JOAN HOBERNICHT

My beautiful, blond, nineteen-year-old granddaughter, Rachel, has a secret. At least she thought she did.

One day as she was bending over to tie her shoes, her jeans slipped down around her hips and her shirt rose up, revealing a delicate pink tulip resting on her right hip. I pretended I didn't see anything, trying to hide my utter shock.

Nice girls don't get tattoos, I thought.

I never mentioned the tattoo during my weeklong stay at her home in Whitewood, South Dakota. Her parents never said a word about it, and neither did I.

Two years later, I received a note that stories were being collected for an anthology about women with tattoos. At seventy-four, my personal experience regarding the subject was very limited. And then I thought of Rachel.

She was in her Mitchell, Michigan, apartment when I called her on the phone. She was shocked to learn that I knew all about her tattoo. She agreed to an interview via telephone from my home in Arizona.

And this is her story:

I never really gave much thought to getting a tattoo. Oh, I'd seen lots of them in Sturgis during rally week, having lived close by in Whitewood most of my life. My parents would take my sister and me down to Main Street one day during the week of the rally. They held tightly to our hands as we gazed openmouthed at the display of tattooed flesh. But those women were so coarse and unrefined, and the men treated them without respect.

"Don't you dare think about getting a tattoo," my mother told us.

My friend Veronica called on my cell phone one day the summer after high school graduation. "Let's go shopping in Rapid City," she said.

I agreed. I had just gotten my paycheck from my job as a bus person in a restaurant in the Midnight Star Casino in Deadwood, and I was ready to have some fun. When walking down Main Street, we passed antique stores, gift shops, and—a tattoo shop.

"Wait, wait, cool!" Veronica said. We stood in the open doorway and watched the artist at work. The customer was getting a big eagle tattoo and every so often we saw him wince.

"Let's go, Veronica," I said, tugging at her sleeve.

"Hello, girls," a nice-looking woman in jeans and a white T-shirt said. "Would you be interested in getting a tattoo?"

"No. Thanks. Just looking," I replied, pulling my friend's arm a little harder.

"What do you have?" Veronica said, pulling free of my grip.

I punched her this time. "Let's go!"

"We have some nice discreet flowers and butterflies you girls might like. They're small but delicate. Harry designs them himself."

We looked at the pictures of tattoos. "It would be fun, Rachael. I like the lavender lily," Veronica said.

"I would want a pink tulip, and I don't see any," I said.

"Oh, Harry designs them himself. Just tell him what you want and he will do a good job," the lady said.

"That's right!" The man called Harry turned on his stool and looked right at me. "Don't believe all the horror stories you've heard about tattoos. I learned all of the rules about tattooing safety and I follow them strictly. I also follow the law, and will need to see both of your IDs if you want to get one. You have to be eighteen to get a tattoo without your parents present."

Both of us produced our legitimate identifications, being careful to hide our fake ones used for beer purchasing.

Harry sported a long black ponytail, but he wore glasses and looked very clean. The entire shop was immaculate. "I use disposable needles and I wear gloves. I can guarantee you won't get an infection," Harry said.

"It doesn't hurt much," the big biker who had just gotten an eagle tattoo volunteered. He left the shop whistling.

Veronica plunked herself down on what looked like a dentist's chair and said, "How much is the lavender lily?"

"It depends on how large, where, and how many leaves you want. But your basic small one will run you about seventy-five dollars," Harry replied. Then he grabbed a pencil and sketch-pad, and drew a lily with a short, bent stem. He penciled in a leaf close to one of the petals and another leaf lower down on the opposite side. Even just in pencil, the flower looked delicate. "This would look lovely on you," Harry said.

"Do it," Veronica said, and she slipped her jeans down below her right hip.

I watched in amazement as the artist did his work. He carefully mixed the paint to get the right shade, and painstakingly outlined the flower before applying the color.

Veronica reclined in the chair and Harry adjusted it to the right height. I gave her sips of her soft drink occasionally, but she held quite still. The entire process took only thirty minutes.

I could hardly wait for my turn. "I really want a pink tulip," I told Harry as I pulled my jeans down on the left side.

"Wait a minute, I need to sketch your flower first," Harry chuckled.

The sketch showed a single dewdrop on one of the tulip petals. Only one green leaf sprouted from the short stem. It was beautiful. "Yes, that's exactly what I had in mind."

Harry did a great job on my tattoo. It stung a little, but I was careful to not let anyone see me flinch. Harry put bandages on our tattoos and gave us instructions on what dangers to look for and how to care for them.

We were quiet as I drove back to Whitewood. I put most of my weight on my right hip to ease the slight discomfort in my tattoo region. I don't know what Veronica was thinking but I was elated. I felt different. My self-esteem was rising as I thought about my secret tulip. Until I got close to home. Then my thoughts took a downturn. *What if Mom and Dad find out? What will they say?*

When I turned into my driveway, I saw my grandparents' car, with the Arizona license plate, in the drive. They were going to stay a week and I was glad to get to see them.

My mother saw the bandage on my hip when she brought towels into the bathroom that evening. I had just stepped out of the shower. Of course, I had to tell her everything. Mom told Dad, but he just teased me a little and told me about some foolish things he'd done when he was young. Then they told me not to tell Grandma!

Sometime after the tattoo had healed, I was bending down to tie my shoes and my grandmother's eyes met mine. I wondered if I had just been busted. But Grandma Jo-Jo is so cool, and she never said a word.

Whenever I feel slighted or insecure, I think of my secret pink tulip and things don't seem as bad after all. I don't know if I will ever get another one, but who knows? If the opportunity arises and I'm in the mood, I just might. Maybe my grandma will get one, too.

Writing this story gave me a chance to communicate more frequently with Rachel. She is a lovely young woman. I am proud to have her as my grandaughter, tattoo and all.

Joan Hobernicht is a retired schoolteacher and grocery businesswoman in Lake Havasu City, Arizona. She writes for enjoyment and reads for the same reason. She enjoys the company of her husband, four children, ten grandchildren, and one grand-dog.

They Don't Teach
This in School

JULEIGH HOWARD-HOBSON

"My kids are going to watch me get this tattoo," I tell Joseph, my prospective tattooist. His eyes, green behind thick, black-framed glasses, flicker. He glances over at my three boys. They look back at him; my middle son smiles.

"We're homeschoolers," I said, by way of explanation.

"Oh. Well, that's cool . . . " Joseph's begins, but I see the doubt lingering.

"They'll be out of your way." I wave toward a set of red vinyl chairs.

"May I see your art books?" my nine-year-old asks.

Famous *Inked Chicks*

Laura Vida began tattooing in 1988 in San Francisco, California. She specialized in reconstructive and restorative cosmetic tattooing. In 1997, she opened Pacific Tattoo, which she sold in 2001. She is currently taking a well-deserved hiatus to raise her small children, but she still stays connected with her art by designing shirts and hopes to return to tattooing someday.

"Oh, yeah, sure." Joseph is wary. Not everyone in this world encounters kids, at least not three at a time. Not here. Not polite ones who like to look at art books when they aren't watching the whole process raptly.

"I like your earplugs," my youngest pipes up.

"Thanks." Joseph plasters a smile on his face, decides that my kids can stay, and—tattoo transfer in hand—gets down to work.

Not that he had much choice in the situation. As home-schoolers, my kids like to see how the real world runs—from backroom tours of grocery stores and faintly urine-smelling pens of animal shelters to intricately decorated spaces of tattoo shops; I take them everywhere.

This particular day was a Saturday and my husband was home, but they wanted to come here to see for themselves how Mommy gets a tattoo.

Homeschooling mom and tattoos. For a lot of people, that's a difficult concept to grasp, a contradiction in terms. "Home-schooling Mommy" means reading classics at bedtime, doing math at the kitchen table, making brownies for the charity bake sale, going to piano lessons, and looking like the ideal, home-schooling mother ought to. And no matter how many classics, math problems, brownies, or piano practices I endure, I'm not a good homeschooling mommy. Not with that . . . ink . . . on my skin. What was I thinking?

Now, I could just simply cover my tattoos and no one would be the wiser. My wardrobe includes long-sleeved shirts and pants. But, I've long passed the point where I would consider doing that anymore. I went to my first punk show in 1979, at the tender age of sixteen. I got home that night, cut my hair into [really bad] spikes, and have never looked back.

I got my first tattoo when I was twenty-seven. It was a wild, spur-of-the-moment decision. My husband (boyfriend at the time) and I were on our way to Tijuana, Mexico. We passed a T-shirt shop with a sign that read, "Tattoos Inside." We couldn't resist checking it out, and I left with a permanent souvenir—a Stray Cats tattoo on my arm.

Over time, I got more tattoos, and I never thought twice about them or my punk image. Not at my wedding, not at the births of our three children. I didn't look back during those first heady years of being a hip mama with my tattoos proudly sported, openly breastfeeding at various cool places in my urban-centered hipster world. There was never a reason for me to rethink my tattoos.

That was, until my babies started to grow.

The hip mama crowd I hung with dissolved into newer worlds of preschools and charter schools and I was—as the only homeschooler—alone. I no longer had a group of breast-feeding, dyed-hair mamas to sit in parks with. I no longer had just a smattering of ink on my skin in comparison to the other moms I met up with. Suddenly, I was different from the women

I sat next to at the park, homeschool potlucks, field trips, and library days.

It's not that there aren't any tattooed homeschoolers out there. There are; there just aren't very many, and we all live far apart. What there are in a lot of homeschooling circles are very proper, very conservative mommies that wear pastels, have inoffensive hair, and wear very, very small earrings.

These homeschooling mommies do not have tattoos. Not even tiny ones on the smalls of their backs—although, in all fairness, I suppose they could be sporting huge ones there since I've never actually *seen* the smalls of their backs, but I don't think so. I am the only tattooed homeschool mother most of them will ever meet.

Not that they know it when they first meet me. Or even the second or third time, for that matter. It—and by "it," I mean the weirdness factor that results from them discovering my tattoos—happens later on. It happens after they have come to know me a bit, after they've seen me at scouts, swimming, potlucks, the library, and the parks—where my boys and I look no different than all of the other moms and kids.

The reveal usually goes like this: I'll be wearing a pair of Capri pants with Converse sneakers, chatting to another homeschool mom, and I'll notice a lull in the conversation. Then "it" happens.

"Is that a tattoo?" my fellow homeschool mommy will say, looking at my leg, with an edgy squeak in the word *tattoo*. She'll smile faintly, but her smile is that smile people put on when a circus clown gets too close to them—one filled with apprehension.

"Oh. Yeah," I'll answer, nonchalantly, pulling up my Capris so she can see the whole piece that the pants had mostly covered. It's a nice tattoo, running from my ankle to my knee—a fully garlanded Harvest pole, decorated with wind-blown ribbons and two ravens sitting on the top. It's very colorful, and it's my favorite of all of my tattoos. But I don't expect the same appreciation from my homeschooling peers.

"Wow . . . um . . . that's . . . um . . . really . . . big," would be breathlessly squeaked in that panicked pitch. "I didn't know you had a . . . tattoo," spoken in tones of confused betrayal. And another easy homeschooling companionship is doomed.

It's an unwritten, unspoken, but inherent fact in this mostly conservative world of homeschooling mommies in which I find myself—mothers with tattoos are not "normal" and can't be entirely trusted. They wonder, if I'd get a tattoo, what other sordid things have I done or would I do? Could they have been mistaken about me?

It's subtle. Very, very subtle. But from that point on, whenever I see that homeschooling mother, she'll act differently toward me. It's hard to put a finger on it, but it's there all the same. The distance, the weirdness, the palpable discomfort. Sigh.

It gets old very quickly and it has become harder to shrug off. Not to the point that I would consider having my tattoos removed or covered, or even that I wouldn't get any more. But what gets harder and older is maintaining this double life that I lead.

There's the real me who goes to art galleries, punk shows, tattoo shops, and cafés. That's the me who has friends—real friends—in bands, magazines, and art showings. Friends with two-inch stretched ears and tattooed bodies. Friends among whom I am not nearly the most outlandish, but who accept me for exactly who I am.

And then there is the homeschool mommy me. Regardless of how I look, this part of me goes to the potlucks and rubs shoulders with the women who carry Bibles in their denim tote bags. And this part of me has to accept the fact that I will always be an outcast in my own circle, even to the most nonconservative of the homeschooling set.

So I walk a fine line, stretched between two worlds. Sometimes they come together well—like my children being able to watch a tattoo artist at work (they loved the experience)—and sometimes they crash and burn with words like, "Um . . . you have *more* tattoos?"

But, as more and more women are getting tattoos, and as more and more women are homeschooling, it's just a matter of time until this thin, lonely path I walk becomes a major thoroughfare. Until then, I guess, I will just keep plugging away—homeschooling, tattoos, and all.

Juleigh Howard-Hobson's writings have appeared in Nesting: It's a Chick Thing, The Knitter's Gift, Hip Mama *and* Home Education *magazine among many others. Her art, in collaboration with her husband, Dave, was displayed at Optic Nerve Art in Portland, Oregon. All three of her children have also been published.*

Living Large, Living Free

JOANNE OLIVER FLANAGAN

I'm forty-five years old and I just got my first tattoo. It's a penguin, on my right calf. My tattoo is in celebration of a milestone, a reminder of a decision that I made, and the incredible journey on which I have embarked. Many people who know me were totally surprised when I got this tattoo. But as I tell you my story, maybe you will agree that this was the perfect choice for me.

I have been overweight for the majority of my adult life. Five years ago, I decided to do something about it and lost over 100 pounds. Unfortunately, I was not able to make the mental adjustments that are necessary to maintain such a dramatic physical change. At the same time, I found myself in a year-old marriage that was coming to an end and I had reconnected with a man that I had dated as a teen.

Over the next few years, this revived relationship grew along with my body. I left my old friends and job, moved to a new state, started a new career, and ignored the weight as it slowly crept back onto my body. I found myself happily married to my old sweetheart and unhappily living in a body that weighed over 270 pounds. Together, my husband and I made the decision to take control of our weight and health together, and commit to a weight-loss program.

It's been almost a year now and it's been quite an experience. In addition to changing my eating and exercising habits, I have had to change my way of thinking. I am not *losing* weight, because we look for things that we lose; I am *getting rid* of the weight. I'm also not comparing my rate of loss to my husband's—I can't keep up with him—or with the bodies of other women. I'm only comparing my new self to my old self, and frankly, I look marvelous!

I have gotten rid of over seventy-five pounds. I joined a gym and I am not embarrassed to go there and sweat. I have made a total physical and mental lifestyle change, and it is amazing.

So, why get a tattoo? Why a penguin, why on my calf, and why now?

A tattoo is a body-altering process and it reflects the body-altering process in which I am already engaged. I decided to mark this permanent change to my weight by making a permanent change to my skin with a tattoo.

Getting this tattoo also coincided with my forty-fifth birthday. While this might be an important milestone for many people, I feel it is especially important for me because my father died of heart disease when he was forty-four years old. I have

Famous *Inked Chicks*

Legendary rock 'n' roll star Janis Joplin was influential because she was the first female celebrity to get tattoos to personify her rocker image. In addition, she got her tattoos from the famous Lyle Tuttle. Her tattoos drew attention from fans before her death, but even more so afterward. Many people got replicas of her tattoos or memorials in honor of Joplin. Today, this kind of celebrity emulation through tattoos is commonplace.

now lived a year more than he did and hopefully, thanks to my decision to take better care of my health, I will live forty-five more.

I decided to get a penguin tattoo for a few reasons. Penguins have been my favorite animal since I was a child, and first and foremost, I wanted a tattoo of something I liked enough to see on a daily basis. As I was researching penguins, it confirmed my decision.

Some of the research showed that penguins once flew through the air but that, after years of adaptation, they now "fly" through the water instead. Susie Green, in her book *Animal Wisdom,* says: "Penguin counsels that change, no matter how radical, is always possible if you are prepared to be patient. We cannot become new people overnight, but if we are prepared to accept that change takes time, and believe in our hearts that the cumulative effect of hundreds of tiny changes are in the end monumental, we can in the end do anything." Over the past year I have made a series of tiny, sometimes daily, changes that have resulted in a monumental change to my body, my health, my attitude, and my life.

The penguin I chose for my tattoo is a chinstrap penguin. They live in large colonies and are among the boldest penguins. For me, the large colonies are representative of the number of people that surround me, supporting me and challenging me to continue my journey. The fact that the chinstrap penguins are bold teaches me to also be bold, outgoing, and to "live large." I considered a swimming penguin design, but finally decided that my tattoo would be of a penguin leaping out of the icy ocean. It represents the leap that I have taken into my new body.

Finally, there were a few reasons for the decision to put the penguin on my calf. I mentioned earlier that I would no longer compare myself or my body to that of others. Before I came to that acceptance, I always compared my own body to others and felt inadequate as a result. I have now come to believe that my legs are something to be proud of—they are mine, they support me, they are big, and they are beautiful. Now I am confident enough to draw attention to them by having a tattoo on my calf.

The final decision I had to make was who to have give me this tattoo. For that, I turned to the Internet. One major require-ment I had was that I be able to continue donating blood plate-lets. I've been a platelet donor for over ten years, giving of my body so that those going through medical crises may have a chance at living. According to Red Cross donor eligibility rules, if I got my tattoo from an artist in Maine, I would be able to continue donating blood.

I began my search and found Jennifer Moore at Sanctu-ary Tattoo in Portland, Maine. I read her entire Web site and followed up with a phone call and then a visit to her studio.

Jennifer is not only a gifted artist, but also a healer with degrees in visual art, psychology, and religion. She's a Master Reiki practitioner and certified transformational breath facilitator. As Jen worked on my tattoo and we discussed my life up to this point, I knew that I had made the right choices in all of my decisions.

I say that this was my first tattoo because I know it is not my last. I was telling Ken that when I reached my goal weight, I wanted to get a tattoo of morning glories. Jen told me that in flower lore, morning glories symbolize recovery and freedom from addiction. She confirmed for me that when I am free from my addiction to food, a morning glory will be the perfect tattoo to celebrate this new milestone.

Joanne Oliver Flanagan *is a special education aide living in a tiny New Hampshire town with her husband (her best friend), their beagle, Buddy, and cat, Nagi. She enjoys reading, traveling, and country music.*

Smart Thinking

HELEN KAY POLASKI

Certain I had heard her wrong the first
time, I pressed my ear more tightly against
the receiver and asked again. "You what?"

"I did it," Lissie replied.

I shook my head. "You did not."

Our middle child's infectious laughter
flowed through the phone lines. As always,
my heart melted. The university Lissie was
attending was only about an hour away
from home, but sometimes the distance
felt like light years. Even though I left mes-
sages several times a week, my fiercely
independent daughter didn't always return
them. Today, as she babbled, I was enjoying
our rare visit too much to let her comment
affect me. While I could have sat on the

phone for hours listening to her—even if she just wanted to laugh and talk nonsense—what our middle daughter wanted most from us was acceptance and that was what she was trying to tell me, but I wasn't hearing. Since she had been born, Lissie had a mighty big need to make it on her own, in her own way.

"Oh, but I did!" she replied. "Wait and see. It's green and it's huge and it's on my . . . well, you'll see."

Lissie knew going against her parents on this particular subject might very well put us into early graves. I grinned. "Yeah, right. Your father and I know you're smarter than that."

"Maybe I'm not as smart as you think," she mumbled, her laughter disappearing.

The tone in her voice made my throat catch. "I don't want to argue."

"Mom, I told you I was going to do it," she answered sharply. "I'm not going to live my entire life doing what you want me to do."

Dumbfounded, I sat on the edge of my bed and let my eyes wander around the room. Photos of our three children—innocent, beautiful children—surrounded me. Why would anyone want to mar that perfection?

Lissie sighed dramatically. "You can see for yourself tomorrow when I get home. Better break the news to Dad that he's got a stupid daughter. I've got to go. I'm going to be late for practice."

Before I could answer, she'd hung up the phone.

When Lissie walked in the kitchen the next afternoon, I discovered for the first time how very wrong a mother can be. It was the arrogant tilt of the chin that gave her away. Guilt, pride, rebellion, joy, and determination all mixed together, giving her an aura of independence. I wanted to cry. Not because of the tattoo I now believed she had gotten, but because at that moment the child we had reared had become her own person. She'd gone against our wishes before, but never when the issue was something her father and I were so adamantly against.

What on earth would I tell her father?

I glanced out the window at my husband. He was bent over, working on the cover to the swimming pool. He worked hard, both at work and at home, to make sure our three children had everything they needed or wanted. I could just imagine his mouth dropping open when I yelled cheerfully, "Come see Lissie's tattoo!"

Tattoo of what?

Startled, I realized that I didn't know what the tattoo was of or where it was or how big it was. My imagination went wild. My God. What *would* I tell her father? I looked back at our nineteen-year-old daughter. Lissie looked the same, and yet I could tell something about her had changed. She was more confident. I couldn't help but wonder if that's what a tattoo did for a person. Did it make them more confident? Is that what the allure was?

"Well, you want to see it?" she asked.

My gaze moved across her face. Thank God she'd been smart enough not to ink that. From there, I moved down to her bare arms—smooth and tanned with a slight bulge in her pitching arm. No sign of ink.

Oh God, I prayed—subconsciously folding my hands over my chest—tell me she didn't get some ugly frog or something on her chest! She must have read my mind, because she suddenly threw her head back and laughed.

"You are so easy! I was only teasing . . ."

Relief surged over me and I threw my arms around her. "I knew you wouldn't get—"

". . . about the size," she finished.

I pulled away. "You *really* got a tattoo?"

Frustrated, she glared at me. "Yes!" She dropped her purse on the floor and sat down on the closest chair, shedding her right shoe in record time. Carefully, she began removing her sock. As she inched the sock off, a tiny, green, four-leafed clover appeared on the inside of her ankle.

I gasped and covered my mouth with one hand. "It's so small!"

"Did you think I'd get some big ugly frog tattooed across my chest or something?"

I looked at her for a moment without speaking. Finally, I nodded guiltily. Her eyes grew wide. "Why would you think that?"

I threw my hands up in surrender. "Why would I think you'd even get a tattoo?"

Famous *Inked Chicks*

Margot Mifflin is a writer whose works have been published in several magazines and periodicals, including the *New York Times*. Margot has a personal interest in subcultures and has written several books that dig into the history of body art and tattoo culture. Her book *Bodies of Subversion: A Secret History of Women and Tattoo* (Juno Books, 1999 and 2001) is the only book of its kind, with a detailed history of women and their influence on the evolution of body art.

"Because I wanted to," she shot back.

"Let's put it this way—I should have known you weren't kidding!" I moved closer. "It's very cute, and it's very small," I said, trying to make it okay in my own head.

"It's my good luck symbol."

If she had to have a tattoo, a four-leafed clover strategically placed on the inside of her ankle was the best I could hope for.

Lissie pulled her foot toward her face and examined the tattoo at close range, gingerly running one finger across it. Satisfied, she held it up to my face.

"See?" she said proudly. "It really is cute, isn't it?"

I nodded reluctantly. While I admit I was still concerned about tainted needles and all the things that mothers worry about that no one else ever seems to consider, I had to admit she had put some serious thought into it.

"What do you think Dad will say?" she asked.

Just then, the back door was jerked open and her father walked into the room. He looked at Lissie expectantly.

"What's that?" he asked, nodding to her foot. "A tattoo?"

Lissie's chin went up a notch as she sat quietly while he bent over her foot. He looked at the perfect little clover on his daughter's ankle and then moved his gaze to mine.

"It's really small," I volunteered.

Whether he took my lead or formulated his own idea at that moment, I'll never know, but what he said paved the way for a much stronger relationship between himself and his middle child. For a long second, father and daughter peered at one another and then very slowly, he nodded.

"Well, Lissie, if you had to do it, small and out of sight was the way to go. Smart thinking."

Lissie nodded and hunched over her foot again, her eyes glistening with unshed tears. Her father was a man of few words. What he'd just said was that he accepted her decision and her independence, and that's all she has ever wanted from either of us.

Helen Kay Polaski is a freelance editor and screenwriter. Her most recent editing projects include The Rocking Chair Reader series, Classic Christmas Stories, and A Cup of Comfort for Weddings. Currently, she is working on a humorous book about menopause.

The Turning Point

DEANA LIPPENS

When I think about my first tattoo, it feels like a lifetime ago. The first time a tattoo touched my life and made its mark on me wasn't a favorable experience for me. I was eighteen years old and newly married, had miscarried a child, and my father threatened to disown me if I didn't marry the man that got me pregnant. We ended up living with my brother in Texas and it was there that I got my first tattoo—a number one with wings, the mark of a biker chick forced on me by my husband—in a dirty, seedy, little place next to a taco stand. I didn't get another tattoo for years after that.

I saved enough money to leave my brother's house and headed for North Carolina. I got a job at the Bowery Club, where I was fortunate enough to meet Tattoo "Miami" Lou and Crazy "Philadelphia" Eddie. They became two of my biggest supporters in later years. I worked with Lou's wife, waiting on tables while Lou was tattooing. I used to hang out and watch the artists as they tattooed many Marines with their bulldogs and USMC logos. Eventually, Lou opened his own tattoo studio in the front window area of a place called Jazzland.

Unfortunately, I was stuck in a cycle of violence and betrayal from my husband and at twenty-three—broke and pregnant again—I was forced to return to living with my brother, who had since moved back to Florida, close to the rest of our family. I worked and saved up enough money to eventually get my own place, but my life remained at a standstill for a couple of years, mercilessly tossed about—like a boat on a stormy sea—by my manipulative husband.

My life finally started to change when I met "Doc" Don Anderson through a mutual friend, and he asked me the big question—did I want to learn to tattoo? It was a different world back then. The old-timers frowned on girls in their business, much less tattooing out of their shop. I was twenty-five years old when I started apprenticing with Don. Once I had learned the basics, I started tattooing at biker runs and private parties but soon I decided I needed a real tattoo job. There were only two shops in the area at the time—Fred's Tattoo in Orlando and Sailor Bill's Tattoo Time in Maitland—and neither of them would give me the time of day.

I tried to open my own shop in Florida, but then I was told that Florida law requires that tattoo artists work under the direction of a physician. I went back to North Carolina to visit Lou and learn about sterility. At that time, Lou was on the

Board of Tattoo Licensing. I took the Sterilization, Sanitation, and Technique Class and got my proof of training in blood-borne pathogens so the doctors would sign for me to get my tattoo license in Florida. I have the second tattoo license ever issued in the Orlando, Orange County area since 1984.

It took a few trips back and forth to complete the course and pass the class. On one of my trips, I filled in at the Tiger's Eye for a short time after the shop manager, Tramp, was killed. This was where I met Ms. Deborah Inksmith (of Inksmith and Rogers). She was the first female tattoo artist, besides myself, that I knew of.

My father cosigned for me to get a loan for $2,000. That's all they would give me, but at the time it seemed like $1 million. It was hard finding someone to rent to me so that I could open a tattoo shop. Finally, I met Mr. Lewis—the only thing he was interested in was that I paid my rent on time. So with the

Famous *Inked Chicks*

Julia Gnuse may not be a familiar name to a lot of people, but it's very possible that you've seen her before. Julia holds the current Guinness World Record as being "the world's most decorated woman," and is tied with Krystyne Kolorful, as they are both 95 percent covered with ink. Julia started getting her tattoos as a way to cover the scars from her skin disorder, porphyria, which causes her skin to blister in the slightest sun exposure. Julia has been on the television show *Ripley's Believe It or Not* and also had a part in Aerosmith's "Pink" music video.

biggest obstacles out of the way—the doctor, the money, and the building—I was well on my way toward opening my own studio, Deana's Skin Art Studio in Orlando, Florida. I remained at that location for almost twenty years, but when Mr. Lewis passed away his wife wanted to sell the building. I didn't have enough money to buy it and Mrs. Lewis wasn't willing to work with me, so I was forced to move.

It was then that I relocated to my current location—Christmas, Florida. I have now been at 25026 East Colonial Drive for three years and plan on staying here as long as I can.

Tattooing was a saving grace for me. Opening Deana's Skin Art Studio enabled me to become strong financially and mentally, and stable enough to divorce my abusive husband. It has enabled me to be my own boss, work my schedule around my son's schooling, and be there when he needed me. Tattooing was the best thing that ever happened in my life until I met my loving husband, George.

I have been a member of the National Tattoo Association since 1986 and have been on the Board of Directors for the Alliance of Professional Tattooists for twelve years. I have produced and executed the Annual Marked for Life Female Tattoo Artists Expo for eleven years and I am already planning the next one.

My own apprenticeship ended years ago, but I never stopped learning. While traveling the convention circuits, I met a lot of great people who became very influential to my progress. Sailor Moses instructed me about pigment mixing and needle making. Jack Rudy helped me improve my black-and-gray wash techniques. Dave Long gave me insight on the technical issues like building and maintaining my machines. I hope they all realize just how much I appreciate them.

I have never stopped learning, but I have passed along what I had gained over the years. I have had several successful apprentices including Mike Wilson, Michael "Canman" Cannistraro, and my own son, Rudy Rudnicki, who now tattoos at Sailor Bill's Tattoo Time. The same Sailor Bill who wouldn't hire me so many years ago.

After tattooing for half of my life, I still get up every day loving what I do. Proud of what I have accomplished in my chosen profession, I look forward to the future. I hope that through producing the Marked for Life Tattoo Expo, I have helped women tattoo artists come into the public eye in a positive light. I still have my first tattoo, but now I wear it with pride. I've gotten many more since then and each one of them tells its own story. But together they tell the story of a woman who, against all odds, was able to rise up against a dominating husband and then make her mark in a male-dominated profession.

Deana Lippens *has been tattooing for twenty-five years and has devoted the past eleven years to promoting women in the business through the Marked for Life Female Tattoo Artist Expo. Deana is also a board member of the Alliance of Professional Tattooists (APT).*

Happy Birthday to Me

BARBARA CLARK

My story begins at our local country club one evening several years ago. I was at a party when one of my friends asked me to go with her to the ladies' room. Once we were in the room, she pulled up her sweater to reveal a beautiful dragonfly tattoo on her shoulder. She had just turned sixty, and her tattoo was in celebration of surviving cancer and reaching a milestone birthday. She told me her daughter had gone with her to be part of the experience.

Several years later I had a Christmas party at my house. One of my friends was preparing to leave, and I was in my bedroom helping her find her coat. As we were talking, she pulled up her shirt and revealed a fleur-de-lis tattoo on her breast. She had it done as an early celebration of her sixtieth birthday, and like my other friend, her daughter had also been with her. When a third friend and her husband went together to get heart tattoos to celebrate their wedding anniversary and her sixtieth birthday, my mind was made up.

I would get a tattoo when I turned sixty, and I hoped my daughter would be there.

Having a tattoo is something I'd never dreamed of. I live in a small city in Kentucky and consider myself fairly conservative. I am a deacon in my church, a community volunteer, and was once married to a doctor. I would never have plastic surgery—I'm just not a risk-taker. In fact, the scariest thing I've ever done is ride in a hot-air balloon. When I was growing up, the only people I knew of who had tattoos were either sailors or circus performers. I graduated from college just before it was hip to be a hippie, and my musical taste was more folk music than funk. (I still prefer listening to National Public Radio when I am driving around in my sedate sedan.) But here I was, actually planning to get a tattoo!

As my sixtieth birthday approached, the planning started. My daughter lives in the San Francisco Bay area and she and her friends began to look for a tattoo parlor where I would feel comfortable. As a result of that search, I was referred to the Web site of a female artist named Sasha, and I liked what I saw. My daughter e-mailed her and then I telephoned Sasha to make the arrangements, but I still wasn't sure what I wanted or where on my body I wanted it. About a week before I was to leave for California, I noticed a magnet on my refrigerator that had an Irish blessing accompanied by a picture of a butterfly and the words: "May the wings of the butterfly kiss the sun and find your shoulder to light on." That was how I decided to get a butterfly on my right shoulder.

I had an entourage of four thirty-something ladies on the evening of my tattooing. I was excited but not really scared. Tattoo artist Sasha put me at ease and was more than willing to let me decide the size and colors to be used on my birthday butterfly. When people ask me if it hurt, I say it felt like sweat bees stinging me. It really wasn't that painful. Sasha allowed photos to be taken and it is nice to have them for my scrapbook. After we were done, and sporting my brand-new butterfly, my daughter and her friends took me out for sangria and tapas.

I must admit that when I looked in the mirror the next morning, I wondered what in the world had I done. Just as I was told it would, the skin tightened like a sunburn and peeled like one too. But now I truly appreciate its beauty. I think of it as the continuation of an ancient art form, and feel proud when I watch programs on National Geographic or the Discovery Channel that feature body art.

After I returned home, my first chance to show my lovely artwork was in Wal-Mart when I ran into two friends. I have been very selective in letting people know about my butterfly but have revealed it in some interesting places, including the parking lot of a Ruby Tuesday, a Weight Watchers meeting at the Baptist Church, in the hotel lobby at our pastor's wedding reception, at a tea room in Farmers, Kentucky, and at the Elks lodge (to my dentist and the leader of the band that was playing that night). When my friend Marsha lost her thirty-two-year-old daughter from a sudden illness, I showed several of my friends during lunch prior to the funeral. After the funeral—at Marsha's house—I decided to show her, too. She revealed that she and her daughter had each gotten a tattoo recently. I was so glad I had told her because it made her laugh on a very sad day.

People have surprised me with their reactions. My hairdresser and manicurist were both stunned but delighted that I did it. A former coworker, one who has done a lot of wild things in her life, was shocked. She told me I shouldn't have defiled my body temple. Fortunately not everyone feels that way. On Easter Sunday, I told a church friend who loves butterflies about mine and now she wants to get one in January when she turns sixty.

My husband, Ron, has been ambivalent about my tattoo because his father had been in the navy and had gotten one. When Ron joined the navy, his father told him not to get one because he would regret it. Ron says he was in the Philippines and in the chair ready to be inked when he remembered what his father had said, and he changed his mind. My stepson and stepdaughter, however, each have a tattoo and their dad has been fine with that. I confess to having always admired theirs.

Reaction from most of my family has been positive, although I can tell my older sister does not approve. And never in million years will I tell my ninety-one-year-old mother. I've done enough things in my lifetime that she disapproves of. But then again, my mother might not be so judgmental after all. I believe it is from her that I have acquired such an open-minded attitude. She has always been accepting of differences, understanding of alternative lifestyles, and forgiving of the transgressions of those she loves. She has been exposed through her grandchildren to ideas that would have raised eyebrows in many older people, but despite that, she continues to maintain a sense of humor about life.

When I'm asked if I would do it again, I say I might get one more tattoo, but I feel the same about having more than two tattoos as I do about owning more than two cats. I love cats and at various times in my adult life I have owned two cats at a time, but I have to confess that I think that owning more than two cats is a bit over the top.

My only regret is that I have been unable to donate blood to the Red Cross. I have been a regular blood donor for several years but have not given since my butterfly arrived. When I go back in the fall, I don't think I will tell them why I haven't been there for a year. I'll just say I have been out of town a lot!

Barbara Clark is a sixty-year-old former teacher, mother of two, and grandmother of three. A "professional volunteer," she loves to read, travel, and work on her scrapbooking. She lives in Ashland, Kentucky, with Ron, her husband of eight years, and their seventeen-year-old cat, Abby.

The Phoenix and the Pirate

BRETT PALANA-SHANAHAN

As far back as I can remember, I've wanted a tattoo. Rebellious yet beautiful, sexual and scandalous, private yet public. A tattoo was just what I needed to make me feel more comfortable and proud of a body that had plagued me with insecurities and doubts.

My mother, the nurse, would have nothing to do with it. "Not until you're eighteen, young lady!" After accusing her of being the cruelest woman on earth, I begrudgingly gave in, vowing to wait her out. After all, even with my fake ID, it would be hard to get a tattoo before I became of age, even here in Rhode Island. But when my eighteenth birthday rolled around, Mom suddenly changed her tune. "Not until you're twenty-one!"

Arrggh! That seemed like an eternity away! But still I waited, longing for the day when that tattoo would grace my skin. When my twenty-first birthday finally arrived, Mom branched into a double-parter. "Not until you're twenty-five, *and* not as long as you're living under my roof."

Sigh.

So one summer night after my twenty-first birthday—in true rebellious fashion—I went out with my friend Raina and I did it anyway. I got my first tattoo. To me it was, and still is, beautiful. I'd spent all those years, waiting for permission, thinking about the perfect tattoo. (There would be no cartoon characters or skulls on this girl!) I finally settled on the word "phoenix" written in ancient Greek, because to me it symbolized the power of change. The new phoenix rising up from the ashes—pulling its body from the past, rising stronger and more alive than before—and leaving its old life behind in a pile of dust to begin again, full of promise and freedom. The phoenix was perfect.

Raina and I went to a tattoo shop up on the Hill, where all the mobsters and bikers would mingle. The shop was smoky, for those were the days when you could still smoke anywhere you wanted to—so smoky that the whole shop seemed engulfed in a fog. The walls were dark red and filled from floor to ceiling with white sheets of paper littered with tattoo art. A girl—who looked to me, in all my maturity, to be about thirteen—emerged from the cloud.

"Yeah. Can I help you?"

"I'm here for a tattoo."

Yeah, no shit, her glaring look seemed to say. "Have you picked something out?"

"I brought it with me. Here, it's the word—"

"Are you sure it's spelled right?" she interrupted.

I nodded.

"Okay then, I'll go in the back and make a stencil." She turned "Bill! You ready?"

A man stepped out of the dark backroom; he was over six feet tall and nearly as wide. An eye patch covered his left eye and he sported a grubby salt-and-pepper beard. Dusty, wrinkled, and worn, he looked like a pirate who'd lost his pillaging privileges and had become a street bum instead.

I hope that's not Bill.

"You ready?" he grumbled.

Okay, I guess this is Bill.

"Ah, yes, I'm ready." I turned to Raina, who gave me a hopeful look. I followed Pirate Bill into the booth.

What the hell am I doing?

"Where you putting it?" he asked.

"On my back."

"Uh-huh. Unzip your pants and sit down." He motioned to an old barber's chair.

What have I gotten myself into? I've stumbled into a porn ring! My mother was right. I never should have done this.

Bill looked at me impatiently. "It's just so I can tuck some paper into your jeans so I don't get ink on them. You don't want ink on your jeans, right?"

"Oh, right." I sat backward in the chair and unzipped my jeans. Bill tucked in a long sheet of paper; the kind you sit on when you're on a doctor's table.

If he kills me, I'll already be on the right type of paper for the paramedics.

The shop girl returned with my stencil and Bill placed it on my skin. He opened the needle and assembled his machine.

My palms started getting moist; suddenly I had an abundance of saliva in my mouth and an overwhelming urge to bolt.

"You ready?"

My mother is going to kill me. This may be the stupidest thing I've ever done, spoke my sensible self. But then my adventurous self chimed in. *Come on, coward. For once, take control of your own destiny. You've always wanted to do this, so do it!*

"Yes, I'm ready." Audacity wins.

And as I sat there—my pants undone, slightly pudgy belly hanging out, arms hanging over a cheap ripped barber's chair, bleeding blood and ink—it truly felt like one of the greatest experiences of my life. Pirate Bill suddenly became an artist, stretching my skin beneath his latex covered hands, carefully drawing the letters and whipping the needles for shading. Though he had certainly done it all before, it was obvious that he cared about getting my tattoo right. *My tattoo.*

When the needles were over my muscle (or as some might call it, fat) the pain was pretty minimal, and when Bill was done working directly over the spine bones I just picked a focal point on the floor and willed the pain away. *It'll all be worth it.*

"All done."

"Really?"

"What? Do you want me to do it again?"

"Ah, no thanks. It just seemed so fast."

"That's 'cause I'm good, Sweetie—been doing this for thirty years, ya know." Pirate Bill bandaged my back and I felt like a bloody, inky pile of leftovers. I couldn't believe I had done it! I was so proud of myself for how brave *and* how stupid I was. Positively giddy, I fumbled with my wallet when paying the girl at the counter. She never smiled. I didn't care—I was reborn, just like the phoenix on my back.

I managed to keep that tattoo a secret from my mother for almost a year. When my dad finally told her, she took it better than I thought. Several years later, one night during dinner, Mom announced that she was thinking about getting a tattoo.

"Don't, Mom," my sister said. "Tattoos are so white trash."

"Mom, I think it's a great idea. I think you'd love it," I chimed in.

Mom hasn't gotten one yet, but I like to think that someday she might.

Brett Palana-Shanahan *is a publishing professional whose stories have appeared in several anthologies. She currently lives in southeastern Massachusetts with her husband, Scott, and daughter, Danica.*

Brett is extremely proud of her collection of tattoos and despite the stares and several company policies, loves to show them off whenever possible.

Fish Out of Water

ANNIE WERNER

As I'm writing this, I know there's a big fish hiding beneath my clothes and, if I were naked, it would be eyeballing me intently. The fish is getting bigger by the day, and occasionally it moves, animated by the life growing beneath—kicks, punches, wriggles, and rolls—from the baby growing in my belly.

The fish is a multicolored (pink, purple, orange, and yellow) koi carp that covers my left rib cage flamboyantly and proudly. It was supposed to have a friend on the right, but as anyone who's been tattooed on the ribs knows, this can be more appealing in theory than in practice.

So the cartoon koi swims alone, the closest of my tattooed menagerie to my unborn child who, when he enters the world, will be greeted lovingly by his two Aussie mums and an array of tattoo dinosaurs, stars, hearts, cats, birds, fish, turtles, flowers, and fruit.

What will he make of this unique family arrangement? I know that children can be insecure and worried by what other kids think of them, and at times I worry that our child will have moments of wishing we weren't so different. But the vision of myself and my partner walking down the street next summer, not only tattooed ladies but tattooed mums, fills me with smiles because I know that children are resilient and, above all, curious.

"What happens to tattoos when you die?"

This particular question—atypical in comparison to the usual torrent of "Did it hurt?" and "What does it mean?"—came from the incessantly inquisitive mind of India, the three-year-old I nannied for two and a half years. At the time, the novelty of this question struck me dumb as I tried to think of a culturally sensitive, age-appropriate response that wouldn't shatter her perception of my tattoos as something more than just a design on my skin. I tentatively asked her what she thought happened to people when they died, and she matter-of-factly informed me that they were either burned or buried, in which case they were eaten by worms. I don't think she quite believed that the worms would cooperate in eating such a large expanse of inky skin.

When I went for my first interview for the nanny job, I'd made an effort to cover my tattooed sleeve of dinosaurs, not knowing how the family would react. I'd become used to taking these kinds of precautions. In my experience, a conversation or some other kind of interaction *prior* to the revelation of the true extent of my tattooed-ness often softened people's judgment of me, and at times even alleviated entirely the presumption that I'm easy, a biker, a troublemaker, crazy, etc. India's sister, Storm, however (at that time, an eagle-eyed four-year-old) was not interested in preserving my cautionary modesty. She had spotted the unusually blue skin peeping out from the bottom of my best, most conservative-looking long-sleeved blouse within a minute of my entering the house.

As I settled in to the customary, polite conversation with her mother—congratulating myself on making what I thought was a pretty fine first impression—I could see Storm staring at the barely exposed, offending wrist. Trying to ignore her inspection, I moved on to answering the customary questions from my prospective employer.

"So, Annie, tell me about your previous experience as a nanny? What kind of qualifications do you have?"

But Storm had more pressing matters to investigate and, recognizing the pattern of question-and-answer, piped up with, "What's that on your arm?" while determinedly tugging at my sleeve.

I had promptly been "outed" as a tattooed lady.

Luckily, the family had no problem with my tattoos. In fact, I think they almost added to the appeal for the slightly unusual family (the girls' names should have been a dead giveaway). The young girls, especially, took delight in Annie-the-tattooed-nanny accompanying them to ballet classes and school reading groups, and I was soon notorious among their fellow toddlers at playgroup and kindergarten class. At their school, I was routinely bombarded with wide-eyed requests to see and touch my colored skin.

"But how did they get there?" the kids would ask. "Do they really stay there forever?"

Famous Inked Chicks

Bettie Page is an icon, very familiar to those in the body art community. Born in 1923, her five-foot-five, 128-pound frame was declared "the perfect figure." Bettie began modeling fur coats, which eventually led to her pinup modeling career. In 1955, she won "Miss Pinup Girl of the World," and received centerfold status in *Playboy* magazine. Today, Bettie's legendary pinup photos are used as the basis for many tattoos on both men and women.

At playgroup, I was approached by tiny people toting plastic dinosaurs, hoping to see if that particular species had been immortalized in ink on my arm.

Their entirely innocent fascination with my colorful arms and legs, so often judged by their parents and other "sensible" adults, was strangely empowering. With no socialization yet dictating their reaction to my dermal decoration, their fascination and delight was refreshing for me, wearied as I frequently was by most people's response of staring and disapproving comments.

"Is that real?" I'm often asked by strangers on the street, clearly wondering why on earth I would do that to myself. Apart from the—sometimes rude, sometimes not—connotations of such questioning, I am usually left wondering about the size of the bubble-gum wrapper that it would require to include such a massive fake tattoo. I suppose there is disbelief for many casual observers that anything so huge would be permanent.

I smile remembering Storm and India's favorite bath time game of enticing me to remove my shoes and socks and place my feet in their bath so they could try to wash off my tattoos. They never tired of that game, just as they never tired of me telling them that the colors and designs lived under my skin, out of reach of their soapy little hands. For them, my tattoos were special—almost magical—and their delight animated my tattooed leg as my little baby now animates the cartoon carp.

My belly-fish jerks, flapping his fins as my unborn baby kicks, and I imagine that they are aquatic kin; my baby swimming in his amniotic world, and the tattoo carp swimming across the stretch of skin on my ever-expanding belly. Perhaps, when the sun shines on my body, the tattoo is like a stained-glass window—the translucent redness of blood-filtered sunlight interrupted by the tattooed skin encasing my body. Perhaps my little baby wonders at this, his window to the world he will soon call home, and perhaps, like Storm and India and all their little friends, he will find joy and magic in his multicolored mums and their animated skin.

Annie Werner is a PhD candidate in the department of English at the University of Wollongong, Australia. She's also a tattooed lady, a clothes designer, and is eagerly anticipating becoming a new mother.

Armageddon and Elvis's Hips

VAL LADOUCEUR

Once upon a time, in a faraway land . . .

Well, no—not really. But in 1965, things were so different from today's world, it might just as well be a fairy tale. In the United States, people of color were still not permitted to sit at the front of the bus or drink from fountains reserved for whites, girls in my Montreal, Quebec, high school were not permitted to take science or drafting as an optional course, and Elvis's hips were banned from TV broadcasts, lest they corrupt the entire world. And into that world walked a Chinese lady wearing one of those timeless silk dresses, with a dragon tattoo circling down her arm from her shoulder to her wrist.

I was a ten-year-old girl and lusted after a tattoo like that with all my heart, for I loved nothing more than causing double-takes from passersby. A tattoo was a deliciously subtle way to do that. But I was only ten and couldn't legally get one until I turned eighteen.

Eighteen! To a ten-year-old, it might as well have been a lifetime.

Disappointed, I pushed the dream to the back of my mind, but I didn't forget about it. I made a point during my tours about the city to find out where the tattoo shops were. Other than the Chinese lady, the only tattoos I'd ever seen were on men, most of them stevedores (dock workers). Old Montreal became a haunting ground for a while, for it was just by the docks, yet still a place where respectable young girls (and tourists) could wander for hours. If I strayed from the respectable center of Old Montreal and off into the lesser-known streets where the stevedores did their after-work drinking, nobody would find it too unusual and I would be relatively safe.

There I found the tawdry little shops tucked away like brothels amid the taverns and bookies. Artwork lined the walls of the shop space: dragons, panthers, roses, hearts, hula dancers, anchors, and "Mom."

At the time, tattoos were *really* permanent. Short of taking a sharp blade to your skin, there was no way to get rid of them if you changed your mind. Many a young man discovered that fact after they'd put "Rosie" on their arm, only to end up married to Edith, who resented the tattoo wholeheartedly.

I discovered that the choices on the wall were not for me. I didn't really like any of them enough to live with them for life. And I certainly didn't like any of them enough to endure the scandal I knew it was sure to cause. Tattoos were not ladylike, and I was assured that I would never marry if I had one. None of these designs were worth foregoing boyfriends. Fortunately, I found out that most tattoo artists would do original work as well, which opened up new vistas.

I spent the next few years toying with designs, drawing them and then putting them aside for months before taking a second look to see if they still looked as good. I did the same with other artist's work for the same reason. I still had time to wait before I was old enough to have it inked on my skin; I might as well spend that time in search of perfection. Though I wanted something feminine, discreet little roses or teddy bears were not going to cut it. I wanted something unique.

On my eighteenth birthday, I had an Aubrey Beardsley spitting cat tattooed on my left wrist. I would probably have garnered less-horrified denouncements if I had robbed a bank. My parents were scandalized, my grandparents more so. Folks on the street took horrified second looks—and I was delighted with the shock value of one tiny scrap of skin, for the tattoo was only about one inch square!

The next work of art came some years after, courtesy of the now-famous Smilin' Buddha studio in Calgary—a bird on a branch that took up my entire right forearm. You would have thought I was a serial killer. My boss, who had never commented on the tiny cat, now forbade me to wear short sleeves to work. I don't think he had actually even noticed the cat, but the bird was a bit in-your-face obvious. When I pointed out that I usually had my hands and forearms in hot water washing dishes, he started dithering about perhaps using some kind of brace or bandaging to cover the obscene thing. After pointing out that the tattoo was not going to fall off or leak into the customer's food, and refusing to cover it up, I was fired.

People would come up to me on the street or in restaurants and helpfully tell me that there were now laser treatments that could remove it for me. Some would ask what prison I had been in. Most just couldn't understand that I *liked* my tattoos. I had spent time and money having them put on and I didn't want them taken off.

It's strange. The world had survived Elvis's hips, segregation was history in the United States, girls were being allowed to become doctors and nuclear physicists, but that bit of painted skin was still going to bring about "Armageddon, Missy! You mark my words!"

I started noticing a trend amongst those who commented on my artwork once the initial shock had worn off. Many of those conversations included the words "always wanted one but never had the nerve." Most of those using that phrase were ladies. Within a few years, the question, "Does it hurt to get one?" started popping up. And before too much longer, a comment on my bird and cat would bring a shy, sly lift of the sleeve to reveal a hidden treasure, discreetly positioned on the shoulder.

My bird's now twenty-one years old. The cat is thirty-three. The world hasn't ended, Armageddon holds off, and Elvis is long gone. Today I look around the mall on a summer's day and see tattoos everywhere, on both girls and boys who look no older than ten. Though there are still many that started life on the parlor walls, more and more are becoming unique and individual works of art. Nobody blinks twice at them, regardless of whether they are the fairly standard rose on the ankle or an entire sleeve of fantastical, multicolored creatures. Vending machines offer temporary tattoos to toddlers and parents do not think it amiss. Tattoos are now almost in the same category as hair dye; few women reach twenty-five without needles inking art on their skin.

I rather miss the shocked looks.

Val Ladouceur, *now fifty-two, lives in Calgary, Alberta, just celebrated a silver wedding anniversary, and spends her time writing, painting, and working various jobs, including running her own small press that she started in 2006.*

Forever Eighteen

CATHERINE LANSER

"You know that's going to last forever, don't you?"

"Mmm-hmm," I grunted, nodding my head. "That's the idea."

"How do you think you'll feel about it when you're old and wrinkled?"

I shrugged. I didn't know, but I didn't really care either. And it really didn't matter. What was done was done and nothing my mom said could change that. The small daisylike flower— no bigger than a pencil eraser with purple petals and a yellow center—had been outlined and filled in with permanent ink, inside my right ankle. I could still feel the sting, something like a bee, but I wasn't regretful and nothing she said would make me feel so.

Or at least I hoped not. I hadn't really thought about the long-term implications of a tattoo, or what it stood for, before I did it. I only knew that I was eighteen, that I could do whatever I wanted, and that a tattoo would be an unconventional way to celebrate my adulthood. I had never considered myself a spontaneous person, but when a friend suggested that we get them, I warmed up to the idea immediately. She said we could drive together to the nearest tattoo parlor, thirty miles from our small town, and I agreed. It sounded like a great idea.

Our minds raced as we discussed our options. What graphic would we choose? Where would we put it? What would people say? I settled on a simple flower head, one even I could draw, and she picked a rose with a thin stem. It was exhilarating and we felt like wild women, even as we reigned ourselves in with practicality. We both decided that it would be best to put the tattoo on our ankle, where it wouldn't be visible to just everyone. We also decided that smaller would be better. After all, it was permanent!

We decided to go that very afternoon so we wouldn't lose our nerve, and in no time we had matching bandages on our ankles. On the drive home, I felt like I had really done something amazing, but wondered what my parents would say. I hoped it wouldn't affect their decision to loan me money for college tuition and considered wearing socks in their presence for the rest of my life. By the time I pulled in their driveway, I had regained my confidence and decided to come clean. I was an adult and they should respect my decision.

I won't say they respected my decision, but rather that they dealt with it. They knew that it was too late to undo what I had done, so they shrugged it off. They had parented eight children before me and this would just be added to my file in the same way they had added all the crazy things my siblings had done to their files. And in the same way she reminded my siblings about their choices, for years my mom would bring up the tattoo as a topic of conversation. She would ask innocently as if she were just trying to understand it. Her questions were always passive on the surface, with the more aggressive agenda hidden just below. Even now, sixteen years later, we still have the same exchange.

"Wow, that's some mole you have on your ankle," she'll say as she squints her eyes looking across the room. "You should really have that looked at to see if it's cancerous."

"It's not a mole, Mom; remember, I have a tattoo."

"Oh, yes, that's right. I forgot."

Over the years, others have weighed in with their opinion on the tattoo as well. Some think it's quite interesting and use nice words to describe it. Someone even once described it as delicate, which I took as a great compliment because it's not an adjective I've ever used to describe anything about myself. Some don't say anything at all, but I suspect they are more open about their opinions outside my presence.

When people ask if I regret it, I can sincerely tell them that I don't. My only wish is that I had a more exciting story to tell about how it came into existence. When I hear others tell me the meaning of their tattoo or how they chose to get it after overcoming some great obstacle, I feel as if my story should be more thrilling. I tell them how I got mine when I was eighteen, with a girl I knew then, but don't anymore. I don't even bother to say something witty, such as, "My tattoo's still here, but she's not." There wasn't any great drama to our separation; we just went our separate ways, in the way people who know each when they are eighteen often do.

In the time since my tattoo was born, there have been more significant changes than that. I've become a real adult—something eighteen-year-olds don't know very much about—faced tattoo-worthy challenges of my own, let new people and places into my life and let others slip away. And through it all, the flower on my ankle has been constant. My skin isn't as youthful as it used to be and I'm still a far way from old and wrinkled, but now I can finally answer my mom's question.

How will I feel about my tattoo when I am old and wrinkled? I think I'll feel just fine. I expect my appreciation for it to multiply as the years take me further and further away from eighteen. I know that because even now when I look at it, I marvel at how I have changed since the day it was put there. I trace my finger along the path of the petals and I remember how young, hopeful, and eighteen I was. I see myself in that enchanted moment, still a child but feeling as if I might be something else, and I am not embarrassed. Everything was possible then and this simple, stemless flower, my timeless companion, will always remind me of that.

Catherine Lanser is a writer from Madison, Wisconsin. Her essay "The Smell of Lilacs" appeared in Stories of Strength, *an anthology to raise funds for Hurricane Katrina relief. "The Great Walnut Caper" appears in Adams Media's* Classic Christmas.

No Apologies

KIM KANE

Being a tattooed woman makes a statement about that person. It means she is in control of her body and knows what she wants. Being a heavily tattooed woman means she isn't to be taken lightly and that she is a force to be reckoned with. It's Amazon—mighty, armored, and beautiful—when you're tattooed extensively.

When people see me, heavily decorated with my armor of ink, they stop what they are doing, drop their jaws, and whisper to their friends. Sometimes they will approach me, and they are always full of questions. "Are those real?" "Did you do all of them yourself?" and, my personal favorite, "Oh, you must like pain!"

And then there's the touching. God, I hate the touching. That may sound harsh, but I don't appreciate random strangers rubbing my arms with "ooh" and "aah." I don't place an uninvited hand on someone's hair, their new car in the parking lot, or on the swollen belly of a pregnant woman, and I just expect the same common courtesy in return. And people actually have the audacity to be offended if I pull away. But why do they touch me in the first place? I think it's because they can't believe it's real; they can't believe that a woman, a girl, a mother, daughter, friend, or family member would do this to themselves.

Negative reactions sometimes bother me; some days are easier than others to handle. I recall one day a few years back when I was visiting a friend in the hospital. I was wearing a sleeveless shirt, owing to the fact that it was the middle of summer, and I had just the tops (elbows to shoulders) of my arms tattooed. As I was walking down the hallway toward the elevator, a very large, very shabby woman dragging her dirty, shoeless child, looked at me and sneered, "*That's* attractive." I was so taken aback, I actually started laughing!

More often than not, though, the looks and stares from other women are in admiration. You can see it on their faces when they say, "Hey, cool tattoos," or "I really like your ink." I mean, what's not to like? They are the definition of beauty, confidence, and freedom. We've done exactly what we wanted to do with our bodies. I think a lot of women want to *be* heavily tattooed, but the majority don't want to *live with* being heavily tattooed. Tattooing your skin to the point of no return is a major sacrifice, but it's a sacrifice to be free. Once you give up your skin, there is no getting it back. I do not blame others for only getting a few tattoos—or none—I can't imagine what it would feel like to have a family that wasn't supportive of me being myself. I'm lucky in the sense that, since I tattoo for a living, I don't have to hide who I am forty hours a week.

Like most gals with extensive work, I didn't get them all at once. I started out with one. It was a *K* on my ankle, done by a friend, with India Ink, a needle, and thread, when I was fourteen. My parents—understandably—wouldn't allow me to get a tattoo, so I took the not-so-smart route of rebellion. After a few months of having the *K* all by its lonesome self, I added the *IM* to it. I can still recall how badly it hurt. Later on, I had my sister write my boyfriend's name on my chest. My parents found out, and I was forced to wear that thing on me until I was eighteen, long after the boyfriend and I had broken up. My first professional tattoo was the coverup. A black moon that I can't stand now, which will also probably be covered up some day.

With the moon tattoo, I caught "the bug" and I caught it bad. I was working at a local fast-food joint and I would take my entire paycheck to the tattoo studio and slap it down on the counter, along with the design I wanted. I never even asked how much they were—I just wanted them done, and I wanted them done now. I wanted them all over me. It wasn't until I started working in a tattoo studio that I had any idea how awesome it really is, and how great it looks, to have *lots* of tattoos. When I first started my apprenticeship, there was a female artist working there. Both of her arms were sleeved and she had tattoos on her chest, neck, and throat. That was it for me. As soon as I saw her, it confirmed what I already knew—I wanted to be covered. Six years later, I am still trying to catch up to her.

Being tattooed—and heavily at that—has taught me a lot of things. I have learned to be confident and comfortable in my own skin. There is no greater waste than a human being who doesn't like herself. It has also taught me to be more understanding with my clients. I don't want them to end up with a shoddy tattoo just because I don't *feel* like tattooing a fairy, flower, tribal design, or whatever. I want them to be comfortable in my work area, comfortable with me, and ecstatic with their tattoo. I feel that a lot of women who are looking to get tattooed often get the short end of the stick, and I'm trying to change that, one tattoo at a time. The most important thing I have learned about being tattooed is that if people can't accept your tattoos, you probably don't want those people around you anyway. My very first tattoo artist told me that, and he was dead right.

In the end, all tattoos tell a story. Mine are no exception, but they are personal to me and those stories are private. However, my tattoos do state to everyone, "This is me, I don't apologize for who I am, and I don't care if I don't live up to your ideals." It's my life, and I'll do what I want with it.

Kim Kane *has been a tattoo artist for six years, and currently works in Virginia with her friend, partner, and husband, Phil Kane. She enjoys reading, drawing, painting, and spending time with her family and pets. Her Web site is* http://nobodyimportanttattoos.com.

A Tale of Three Tattoos

HOLLY JANELLE

I can't say which one of my tattoos stands
out the most to me, because each one has
relevance to a different time in my life. I began
this journey when I was eighteen years old
in New Orleans, by picking a piece of flash
off the wall. Looking at each tattoo, I can tell
you who I was with when I got it, what music
I was listening to, and who I was dating at
the time. You would probably think I have
a body full of art by saying this, but no. I
currently wear ten pieces—none of them very
large—but each contains a piece of history,
a story of my past. I can't share all of them,
but I will share the ones I have found to be
the most interesting.

The first tattoo that attracted the most attention—albeit negative—is the bar code on my right arm. One of my best friends and I wanted to get tattoos together. He chose the bar code from the book *Brave New World*. To match, we both got the bar code on our arms, but to keep them unique, the digits on mine ended one number higher than his. As soon as people saw the bar codes, they would tell tales of Revelations and the end of the world when all people were going to be emblazoned with the "mark of the Beast," which, to my new acknowledgement, was a bar code.

I vividly remember standing in line for the bathroom at a club in Louisiana, when this perfect little blond mini-Barbie grabbed my arm as if she were holding on for dear life. The look in her eyes was priceless. While clenching my arm at the tattoo she asked, "Do you believe in Satan? That bar code is his mark." With the biggest smile I could muster, I couldn't resist replying with, "He is my father." Needless to say, I didn't see the girl again for the rest of the night. By no means was I serious, but I had truly had enough of people judging this tattoo. Today, people do not seem to react so apocalyptically to the piece.

One that brings back fond memories is the tattoo I got with my husband, just before we were married. I wanted something special that would symbolize our bond going into our marriage. What better than kanji? I saw the kanji character for "promise" or "vow" and thought it would be perfect. Of course, I wanted a special place for it that would only hold significance for us, like our own little secret bond. To this day, the only people who have seen it are the artist, my husband, and my gynecologist. Perhaps this was my rebellious tattoo because of the placement. It was exciting to be in the artist's chair having it done, and even now it is exciting because it is the one that no one really knows about. Most of my other tattoos are visible when I want them to be.

Throughout my tattoo experiences, I felt I was making my mark as an individual. I truly did not care if other people liked them or not—this was my body and my art. I always considered myself a bit of a renegade anyway, as I was always doing something that was not considered "normal" or "mainstream." I remember my mom telling my younger brother that if he ever came home with a piercing or a tattoo, he would have to move out and support himself. Needless to say, after he got his first piece, he used strategically placed towels and shirts draped over his shoulder to cover it so she wouldn't find out. When we talk about this now, I find it funny because she never told *me* not to get a piercing or tattoos. I asked her why, and she said, "Because you're a girl and girls should know better than to do something like that." How I love that statement.

Of course I am a girl; I'm also a woman who has never felt quite comfortable in her own skin. I have never truly felt like I belonged anywhere. I am not the typical beauty with a great body, great hair, or the prettiest face. Having these tattoos has allowed me to find something on my body to be proud of. I even find them a little sexy. I don't hide behind my tattoos; I'm an open and honest person, with an offbeat sense of humor, who finds unconventional beauty a miraculous thing. By no means do my tattoos define who I am. They may, however, help me start a conversation when I would otherwise be inclined to keep to myself. I consider them marks of beauty that I have chosen for myself.

The most recent tattoo I got holds more significance in my life. After graduating from nursing school, my best friend and I designed our own tattoo to signify our achievement—the letters *RN* and a caduceus, the medical symbol, which represents the new path we have both taken in our lives as nurses. My friend also celebrated another milestone with this tattoo, as it was her first piece of living art.

Now I am more open about my tattoos and have no qualms about getting any of them, even if the situation in my life at the time was nothing to brag about. My family has, slowly but surely, become more accepting of my tattoos, and my mom is even trying to decide what her first one will be. What an experience that will be, considering it took her fifty years to get a second hole in her ears. For me, I have plans to continue what I started many years ago. With each new piece of art, I emerge a little more from my cocoon.

Holly Janelle is twenty-nine years old and lives in Ridgeland, Mississippi, with her husband of seven years, their two dogs, and five cats. She works as a psychiatric nurse, and her favorite artist is Rusty at Eternal Body Art in Jackson.

Moving Forward

JULIA M. SHEA

Sitting in the chair (which, appropriately
enough is the same as a dentist's chair)
watching the artist prepare her needles,
I'm struck with an intense fear so powerful,
I can barely keep from kicking her in the chin
and making a break for it. Kind of in the
same way a woman who is pregnant with her
second child forgets the pain from her first
pregnancy, I forgot the pain from my first
tattoo. But this time, it would be like having
triplets, because the tattoo I was getting was
three times the size of the first one.

I glance at my friend Rick getting work
done on the snake on his bicep. It annoys
me that he's happily chatting up the artist,
who is repeatedly poking him with a really

sharp needle. Rick notices my apprehension and smiles. "Don't worry about it. You're fine. You're in good hands with Donna."

"Yep, it won't hurt a bit," Donna says as she dips the needle into the ink which, when you think about it, looks just like the drill dentists use to dig out cavities. I frown at Donna. "I know better than that."

She laughs, "Well, it's going to hurt more when we get down to the ankle bone. Not much padding there."

Great, I think. It hurt bad enough the first time when all the ink *was* on a more fleshy part of my leg. My best friend, Katie, is sitting in the chair next to me (wisely *not* getting a tattoo). "This is going to be fun."

I glare at her. "Nice way to be supportive."

Donna begins her work. I cringe and dig my fingernails into the palm of my hands. "I'm sorry," she says, "but we have to get a lot of ink in here to cover up the other one so it doesn't show through. It's going to hurt a little."

The tattoo Donna is covering is a heart so small, people mistake it for a birthmark, which is ironic considering I got it to make me feel tough. I've always been a little intimidated by people with tattoos, and I wanted to have that kind of effect on people. I suppose, subconsciously, I had hoped having one would make me stronger.

"Thanks for the warning." I try to smile as she continues the assault on my ankle. Searching for distraction, I remind myself why this second tattoo is necessary. First, I really do like them; it's one of many ways to express your individuality. Thinking about that, I glance at Rick again and try to figure out what part of his individuality the cobra swallowing up half of his arm is expressing. I decide that I don't want to know.

The main reason this tattoo needs to be covered up is because it was something I had done with an ex-fiancé. I didn't want the reminder of his infidelities or the woman he left me for after moving me 500 miles away from my home.

I am determined to make this tattoo a more positive experience, especially since I will never be able to get rid of this one without an amputation. Rick is the perfect person to have with me, because he was the one who put me back together after my breakup. He held me when I cried about it, but would also point out my own role in the relationship's demise. He made me laugh and distracted me from the pain, while making sure I understood that I was a spoiled brat and if I thought about someone other than myself once in a while, I might not be crying all the time. He was great at keeping me grounded.

The machine buzzes over my anklebone. I jump, every muscle in my body tightening into knots.

"Sorry."

"It's okay."

"Hey, this is nothing as far as pain goes," Donna says. "You should have your breast tattooed."

Rick's artist looks over at us. "That's nothing. Try piercing your scrotum."

My eyes grow wide with horror. "You've got to be kidding." I feel like a virgin at the local swinger's club. "You can do that?"

"Let me see." Katie jumps up from her chair. I grab her arm. "Oh, no you don't. Sit down."

Donna giggles and reaches into a drawer in her cubicle space. "Here, take a look at these."

Katie pulls her chair close to mine and we start paging through books of tattoos and body piercings. I gasp at a pair of breasts with vines and flowers joining them in a garden of

Famous *Inked Chicks*

Amy Brown was born in 1978 and is a relatively new artist, breaking out into the art world in 1993 with her depictions of exotic fairies and friendly dragons. She became wildly popular, practically overnight, and became an instant hit with tattoo enthusiasts. Her paintings became the subjects of countless tattoos, and her Web site even has an entire gallery dedicated to these inked homages to her art that have been submitted by her fans.

color. Katie shivers when we see what looks like Chinese characters on someone's ear. The book serves its purpose—I am sufficiently distracted and Donna finishes my ankle without any additional flinches on my part.

"All done." Donna sits back and crosses her arms over her chest, examining her handiwork. "Looks pretty damn good. Can't see the old one at all."

I look down to see the butterfly and rose delicately working their way up my ankle. They are beautiful and I smile at Donna. "Thank you. It looks great." I'm glad I didn't kick her in the chin.

I know this is a turning point in my life. Every time I look at this new tattoo, I will see the distance I've traveled and the growing that I've done. I will always be reminded that I am not a bad person who doesn't deserve love so much as I am a person who has made some mistakes and needs to give people a break.

I have to admit, I do feel pretty tough with this tattoo, even though the design is about as feminine as you can get. I like feeling that I might intimidate some people a little bit. I feel tough enough to handle anything, to be different, and to stand out in the crowd. From this day on, I am moving forward and creating my own path.

Julia M. Shea graduated summa cum laude from Mount Mary College in Milwaukee, Wisconsin, with a BA degree in professional writing. She lives in Milwaukee with her husband, John, and their two cats. Visit her blog at http://jgwriter.blogspot.com.

First Impressions

CHRIS MAREK

I can recall, very clearly, the day my mother found out about my tattoo. We were spending the day looking at wedding dresses and came upon one of those hotel ballroom extravaganza sales. Brides-to-be were packed like sardines into multiple temporary dressing rooms.

I was invited to join a group willing to share some of their space in their curtain-protected cubby. I declined at first, stating that I was in no hurry and could wait for an empty spot. Mom pressed me to go in and get started, commenting that she never knew me to be shy before. I hesitated one moment and then came to a decision. *She's going to find out about it eventually,* I told myself. *Might as well get it over with now.*

"I've done something you're not going to like," I said, and I asked if we could speak about it privately.

Mom wasn't feeling up to playing games. She told me to just spill the beans, so I begrudgingly admitted that I had a tattoo on my back.

"Well, that was stupid," she answered, and then she shoved me back into the dressing room and told me to get changing.

That was about the extent of what I had dreaded for over a year. What Mom didn't realize at the time was that she was actually seeing my third tattoo. The other two were hidden. Even more surprising was her next encounter with my newest ink.

My cousin's wedding approached and I was proudly wearing a rather girly dress with heels. By now my family knew of my tattoos and had adapted to my husband's sleeve. I was also sporting two new complimentary ankle tattoos of a demon and angel ducky. Again, I was nervous. Finally, after sitting in the church pew for about half an hour amongst family, I flat-out

Famous *Inked Chicks*

Amy Krakow's affiliation with the body art community was based mostly on her position as producer and promoter of the Coney Island Tattoo Festival for over a decade. Her most prominent influence, however, was her book, *The Total Tattoo Book* (Warner Books, 1994), which contains a wealth of information about tattoo history, celebrities with body art, and general tattoo knowledge. Much of this book has since been outdated, but it still remains a valuable resource.

asked my mother what she thought of the new ink. She told me they were very cute and said she always knew that I would get more, she just didn't realize how many more. To give her proper credit of official mother status, she did end the conversation with, "but did you have to get two?" There was the mom I knew.

Now my entire right arm pays homage to our feline friends. This was a progression that I'm not sure I ever saw coming, but would never undo. I started with one beautifully feminine new-school-style kitten and crossbones piece on my upper arm, but always considered taking it to at least a half sleeve. I rationalized that even with two half sleeves, I could fully cover my work and look "normal."

I must admit, though—that half sleeve was where I felt that I had crossed an invisible line of truly being inked. It was my ninth piece, but somehow it made me feel like there was no turning back. Women everywhere have dainty, sexy tattoos on their ankles, shoulders, and the smalls of their backs. But an arm tattoo was something anyone could see, even if I wore pants. It was something that peeked out under most short sleeves.

I was fortunate that my employer made no effort to deter me, which really made me both happy and relieved. In the beginning of my seven-year employment, my own manager displayed an eyebrow piercing and made me comfortable enough to begin wearing my labret. The tattoos of my husband, who worked part-time in the same office, were accepted without question, though I still started off with every effort to keep myself covered.

Tattoos can be a very private thing and even though they are technically "on display" doesn't mean you want to be bombarded with commentary or questions. They are not access to an open forum, contrary to what many people believe. After feeling secure with my family and friends, the one kitten and crossbones piece increased to two. Not long after obtaining half-sleeve status, I realized that I was not done. More inspiration surrounded me and I surrendered. My family and work continued to be supportive and kind as my full sleeve became complete.

My right arm sleeve was completed over the course of three years. Two artists contributed to the final product. Both are remarkable artists and one has become a very close friend. I have moved away from Texas and hold a new job as an office manager for a corporation in Las Vegas, Nevada. I arrived with at least one week's worth of proper business long-sleeved shirts. While the new office was aware of my ink, I am always hesitant of first impressions and want people to get to know me before they pass judgment based on my ink alone. Considering that the vice president of the company displays a tattoo shop bumper sticker on her office door—a shop belonging to one of her relatives—I have since traded in the long sleeves for sleeveless tank tops. Vegas does have record 115-degree temperatures, after all.

I don't experience much negativity in my life because of my tattoos, nor do I feel that they limit me in any way. It has been my choice to not extend anything onto my hands or neck, but that is merely a personal decision and I do not judge those who choose otherwise.

People frequently question what I intend to do with my other arm, which remains undecided. I know I will ink it, too, but I think these things out carefully. I respect the permanence of tattoos enough to plan them out until I am completely locked into knowing what I want. The cat arm came together with extreme ease and it always felt right. I expect no less for my right arm.

Now when my mother waits with my husband and me for a table at a restaurant and she sees someone staring at us—or even worse, rudely talking about us—she pipes right up and says, "Oh, I see you notice my daughter and son's tattoos. Aren't they amazing?"

Chris Marek is thirty years old and has been married for eight years. Her tattoo artists include Eric Inclan, Chris Merchant, Tim Creed, and Mark Thompson. Chris enjoys attending tattoo conventions, reading, writing, and her cats.

Tattoo Fever

TARA ALTON

I had told myself I wasn't going to get any more tattoos. Surely, I didn't need more of them. Over the last ten years, I had collected twelve of them, including an old-school sailor Jerry girl, a Georgia O'Keefe inspired sunflower, a sexy angel fish with a purse, and the queen of all pinups, Bettie Page. Every one of my limbs sported one or more tattoos, not to mention my belly and the back of my neck.

When I was first tattooed, I couldn't wait to show them off in public. I was a Metro Detroit suburban girl working as a travel consultant—basically a working stiff with a crummy little cube and a strict dress code—and I wanted to show the world outside work that I was in control of my body. This was how I chose to express the wild child inside me, but as the years passed, I found I had developed more of a love/hate relationship with my tattoos.

I still loved them in my personal time, but I was tired of the stares from little old ladies at the supermarket who thought I was a criminal, a biker chick, or just plain insane. I knew that in this day and age I shouldn't let it bother me, but sometimes, it did.

There was another reason I didn't want any more tattoos as well. My favorite tattoo artist had passed away unexpectedly, and my desire to continue collecting them seemed to have died along with her.

That was why, when I went to the Motor City Tattoo Expo in Detroit with my friend, Hank, another avid tattoo collector, I thought I was completely safe from tattoo fever. Hank had wanted to go to buy some new tattoo T-shirts, a major staple in his wardrobe, and I thought I might be able to find some cute Bettie Page stuff.

The expo was being held in the Marriott in the Renaissance Center. The building had to be one of the most confusing ones I had ever been in, and I was pretty sure we were never going to find the expo as we scoured the circular towers with a floor plan that could make anyone feel dizzy. One minute we were looking at the view of Detroit. The next minute we were staring over the Detroit River at Windsor, Canada. Finally, we found a security guard who pointed us in the right direction.

After we paid our admittance fee, we entered the huge ballroom with wall-to-wall booths of tattoo artists from all over the world. Here, no one was going to give you a dirty look because you had a tattoo. For the first time in months, I felt like I was accepted. I had no problem walking up to tables with heavily tattooed guys with skulls and evil clowns adorning their muscular arms and checking out their portfolios.

I still thought I was going to be safe from tattoo fever, because the alluring call of the tattoo machines hadn't even triggered a response from me, which it usually did, like a sailor being drawn to the seductive Siren's song. Nor had I seen any artwork that really spoke to me.

Using my mad money, I bought a cute pink tank top with "Miss Bitch" written across the front to wear around the house and some Bettie Page lapel pins. We were going to make one more pass around the floor and go get some lunch in Greek Town when we came around a corner we hadn't visited yet.

And then it happened. Tattoo fever hit me.

My gaze froze on the artwork adorning a booth. Sacred Hearts. Bold, bright colors. High Drama. Unable to walk away, I started flipping through the artist's flash sheets and portfolio. A guy manning the booth told me she was a female artist from England, and she would be back in fifteen minutes because she was finishing taking a seminar.

I couldn't believe how her work was knocking me for a loop. The designs clearly had an old-school style, but she had reinvented them with her own flair and vision. If I was going to be a tattoo artist and if I could draw, this would be exactly the type of work I would do.

On a page of her flash, I spotted the cutest little swallow in blue with an orange and yellow underside. It was holding a tiny green twig and I could have sworn it winked at me. My heart went pitter-patter. Was this love at first sight?

Feeling a little dizzy, I made myself walk away from her booth. I could be smitten with the little bird and still not get a tattoo, I thought. I didn't need a thirteenth tattoo, did I?

I walked around the expo with Hank, trying to shake off the clutches of tattoo fever, but the thoughts kept racing back me. If I got the little blue swallow, where did I want it placed on my body? I didn't want any more tattoos that I couldn't conceal. I thought about it on the back of my shoulder, but I'd never get to see it unless I looked in the mirror, much like the tattoo on the back of my neck.

Therefore, I decided I might want it on the right side of my chest, near the front of my shoulder, but it depended on what this artist was like as a person. If someone was going to tattoo me, I wanted to feel the right connection.

Fifteen minutes had passed. Hank knew where I was going the moment I said I wanted to go back. The moment I saw her, I knew I was done for. She was in her early thirties, petite, and cute as all hell. She had jet-black hair tucked into two pigtails, facial piercing studs, and a sacred heart tattoo nestled in her cleavage. She was wearing cat eye glasses, a pinstriped, fitted blazer over dark blue jeans, and a big clunky chain necklace with a star at the center. There was a henna-style tattoo on her hand and she was totally British, which, to my Anglophilic obsessions, was a dream come true.

As I talked to her about the little blue swallow, I felt like I was standing outside my body. I told her I wanted some little stars trailing off the bird. She made the stencil with the stars. Hank quietly slipped me a loan until I could get to an ATM.

Unfortunately, I had worn my baby T-shirt with "pirate girls kick ass" on the front and a foundation garment bra beneath. I hadn't planned on stripping off my clothes at a tattoo convention. In fact, I'd never even been tattooed at one of these things before.

I ran to the bathroom, deciding to sacrifice my new "Miss Bitch" tank to the cause. When I came back, I was sans bra, my tattooed arms not covered up, and I felt freer than I had in a long time.

Pushing down the strap of my T-shirt and placing a paper towel over the fabric, it took her no time at all to place the stencil on my skin and get to work.

The moment the needle hit my skin, I asked myself if I was completely nuts. This was a total impulse tattoo. Usually I took months to decide on a design. Why was I doing this? Was there something wrong with me? Was I going to regret this?

The single needle pain seemed to stab through my shoulder. Did it hurt this much last time? I couldn't remember. Get into the tattoo zone, I told myself. I looked up at her posters, listening to the loud rock 'n' roll music blaring from the nearby speakers. I wasn't breathing. I took a breath and let it out. My thoughts zoomed around inside my head like a pinball in a game.

I glanced at her. She was so close to me that I could smell her shampoo. Why was I letting this woman hurt me for money? *Breathe.* This really hurts. *Breathe.* Why don't they turn down the music? The back of this folding chair was killing my back. *Breathe.* She had a tribal swirl black tattoo on her neck. How cool was that? This little swallow design was so freaking cute. People I didn't know were watching me get tattooed. *Breathe.*

I glanced over at Hank, who was watching me. There was a knowing look in his eyes as well as a small smile on his lips. He knew a tattoo addict when he saw one. After all my declaring I was getting no more tattoos, here I was, once more, under the needle.

Taking a peek at my right front shoulder, I could have sworn the little blue swallow winked at me from my own skin, and I knew he was right.

Tara Alton lives in the Midwest, where she works as a travel consultant. When she is not working or writing erotica, she collects tattoos, worships Bettie Page, and plans new adventures into the world.

Grandma Led the Way

MICHELLE SWARTZ

I called my grandmother to congratulate her on becoming an octogenarian. Being a basically self-absorbed person, I was calling her a few weeks after her birthday. "So, what'd ya do for your birthday, Grandma?" I asked, expecting to hear that she and some of her Red Hat Society friends went to the all-you-can-eat buffet for lunch.

"I bought a red sports car convertible," she replied blandly.

"You did what?" I yelled into the phone.

"I traded in my white sedan car for a red sports car convertible with red leather seats." (I found out later that it really was a two-door coup with a sunroof, but Grandma thought it was a sports car because it didn't have four doors, and it was red with leather seats.)

"Why did you trade in your car, Grandma?" I queried amazedly, a bit concerned about my grandmother's mental state—not to mention my inheritance.

"Because I always wanted one," replied my grandmother with great equanimity; she was enjoying freaking me out. No one ever described my grandmother as calm, reserved, or unassuming.

After we had thoroughly discussed every detail about how she went to the Ford dealership the morning of her birthday because her brother still worked there two days a week and could get her a deal, and how she had been thinking of getting a new car for some time because her white sedan was old, even if it still did look nice because she always parked it in the garage, I asked "So what'd ya do to celebrate your birthday after you got the car, Grandma?" still expecting to hear about how she and her church friends went to lunch.

"I drove downtown and got a tattoo," was her reply.

"You did what?" I yelled again.

Again with unnatural equanimity masking sheer joy, she replied, "I drove downtown and got a tattoo." I had a lot of questions, the first one being where, and the second one being what and how big. The "where" was not so bad, considering my grandmother had retired and didn't have to worry about impressing future employers, and I wasn't surprised by the "what." The "how big" answer, though, was a bit disconcerting.

My eighty-year-old grandmother had her right forearm tattooed with a five-inch pig—which looked somewhat like a female Porky Pig sans jacket—with a rose in its mouth like a tango dancer. Now, my grandmother collected pigs—not real pigs, but figurines and anything with a pig on it. She had a pig toilet brush holder, a pig mailbox, pigs embroidered on all the towels, and shelves and shelves of souvenir figurine pigs from everywhere she had ever been and from everywhere her friends had ever been. No one knew how many pigs she actually had. Children always gave up counting them, even when they were promised $20 if they counted them all. In Bermuda, there are pigs on their pennies. When my grandmother visited there, she brought a big jar of Bermudian pennies home; she would give guests a "pig penny" as they walked in. So in retrospect, it was natural that my grandmother, who was already known as the "pig lady," would get a five-inch pig tattooed to her forearm.

After we had gone over every detail of the tattoo—how clean the shop was, how friendly the staff was, how nice they all said it was that she was getting a tattoo for her birthday and that it didn't hurt at all—I asked, "So, Grandma, why did you get a tattoo?"

"Because I've always wanted one."

I had always wanted a tattoo, too. Ever since I was a little girl and saw my dad's navy buddy flex his triceps to make his tattooed American eagle's wings flap, I had wanted a tattoo. But my mom said you could get a disease from getting a tattoo because tattoo parlors weren't clean and they used dirty needles. As a self-absorbed person, I am very germ conscious—borderline germ phobic, in fact—so I basically decided at age four that I would *never* be getting a tattoo. But my grandmother, who had been a surgical nurse, was not concerned about getting a disease from her tattoo.

I waited a few months, dubious. Grandma's arm did not become gangrenous. Grandma remained healthy, running around the Valley of the Sun in her red "sports car" with the sunroof open, having a ball and showing everyone—from the grocery store clerk to the people in line at the post office—her tattoo. She conveniently wore three-quarter-length sleeves most of the time so you could easily see the tattoo, but you couldn't see all of it unless she rolled up her sleeve.

My thirtieth birthday was approaching too quickly. How was I going to mark the momentous occasion? I really wasn't looking forward to it, because I still hadn't accomplished many of my life goals, so a big party was out of the question. Then, of course, I had that flash of realization: *If my grandmother, a surgical nurse who still reads medical journals about bowel reconstructions, can safely get a tattoo at age eighty, why shouldn't I get a tattoo at thirty?* After all, Grandma said it didn't hurt.

Grandma either lied or people lose nerve sensation when they become octogenarians. Getting a tattoo did hurt, a lot. There were tears in my eyes every time the tattoo artist took a break to refill the needles. I said a little prayer of thanks and for endurance each time he did. Because I still periodically have to impress future employers, I wanted to get a part of my body tattooed that I could hide if necessary, but could also show to the world when I chose. I had a three-inch-long Celtic cross tattooed above my right ankle.

As I've grown older, my Christian faith has become increasingly more a part of who I am, so I was, and still am, confident that Christianity is a part of my personality that is very unlikely to go away. I decided a cross was a good symbol to put on my body, because it expresses who I am and what I believe. If for some reason I die a horrible death and my body is mummified and found by archeologists thousands of years later, then at least people will know that I was a Christian.

I wasn't expecting getting a tattoo to be any kind of a learning experience, but the ugly truth about what a self-absorbed person I still am was painfully and glaringly self-evident as I lay on the tattoo artist's table. Jesus was flogged and died on a cross, and there I was crying because I was getting a few needles stuck in my lower calf.

When children ask me about my tattoo, which is more visible than hidden these days since I'm a stay-at-home mom, I tell them, "You have to be at least thirty years old to get a tattoo because you won't change your mind so easily about what you want, and getting a tattoo hurts a lot—I cried even though I'm a grownup."

My grandmother enjoyed her tattoo for five years before she passed away. I'm grateful that she gave me the courage to get a tattoo and enjoy it for (hopefully) much longer than five years. My mother is mortified that both her daughter and her mother got tattoos; she says that, in her case, "lunacy skipped a generation."

But if my grandmother hadn't gotten a tattoo, I wouldn't have had to opportunity to share this story and to pass on her memory to all who read this book. Maybe I'm not as self-absorbed as I used to be.

Michelle Swartz is Mildred Mosley's oldest grandchild. Michelle has worked as a technical writer in Silicon Valley and copywriter in Bermuda. She currently lives in San Jose, California, with her husband and infant son.

Beautiful Pain

SAMANTHA JUNE ENGBERS

In today's society, we are conditioned to hate our bodies. The shape, the size, the color—we hate it all, because of this deeply ingrained idea of perfection. Magazines, TV, and movies have created a Brave New World of beauty, a place where anything that is not perfect is immediately removed. I know this for a fact, because I was one of the millions of women to fall into this trap. At eighteen years old, I already hated my body, or at least I did, until I decided to claim it back.

Since late elementary school, I have despised the way I look. I was teased for being chubby, for my pouffy hair, and my eclectic style. This cycle of teasing and self-loathing transferred straight into high school.

I thought the move would give me a newfound self-confidence, but I was so wrong. Going to school in a wealthy neighborhood of well-dressed, beautiful people, I felt so out of place. I found all sorts of reasons to hate my body, and fell into a depression.

I hated going into public, hated social situations, and began taking out my hatred on my body. I started doing what many young girls with displaced anger do to their bodies. I began cutting myself. My wrist, my legs, my arms, my stomach; no place was left untouched. I hid the marks from the world, bandaging them up, sinking deeper and deeper into the hole of depression. My parents and my friends knew, but they did little to stop my problem. A few words here, a scolding there, but that was all.

By the middle of high school, my problem was at its worst, and the teasing reached a boiling point. My first boyfriend dumped me, saying that no one would ever love me. My "friends" turned against me. I would sit in my room and feel sorry for myself and throw all of my anger into my body, or into my paintings. There were only two things that made me feel better—my self-inflicted pain and my art. I felt horrible. I had to do something. I had to change.

When graduation came around, I began to look toward the future. I hoped university would be the escape from all this, from the torture and self-abhorring. Perhaps I would be able to love myself again.

The summer went by in a blur. I started to claim back my body through piercings. The pain offered a release, and the metal adornment added to my self-confidence. I cut my hair short, pierced my nose, got a Monroe, pierced both of my nipples, and slowly started to like myself again. But in the back of my mind, I still felt inadequate. I was still chubby, and now scarred all over.

That September I started university, and it changed me. As an outcast artist at my high school, I was embraced with open arms by like-minded people in my program and in my residence. They were all like me. Because I lived in a fine arts building, everyone was an actor or a painter, a dancer or a musician. And all of them had stories like mine. They were troubled, different, and just a little bit weird. They knew what is was like to be an outcast, and we all bonded immediately. We became a family and for the first time in my life, I began to feel at home, at peace with the world. My strange ways were praised and my unique appearance admired. I began to feel comfortable in my

Famous *Inked Chicks*

Jacci Gresham is a rarity in the tattoo world. She was quite possibly the first, and for quite a while was the only, African American female tattoo artist. Jacci also prevailed over the prejudice of her own boyfriend and business partner (at the time), tattoo artist Ajit Singh, who established a rule not to allow female clients because he felt that it was inappropriate for women to wear tattoos. Jacci revoked this policy and now says that her female clients represent about two-thirds of her total business. Ms. Gresham had two studios in New Orleans, one of which was damaged beyond repair during Hurricane Katrina. She has relocated to her only remaining shop, Aart Accent, in the French Quarter.

own skin. After eighteen years of hating my body, I began to accept it.

But still, I wanted to claim it back for good. Instead of marking it with the scars of hate, I wanted to cover it with art, something I had always loved. I wanted to make my body its own piece of art. My birthday was coming up, and my new amazing friends gathered money together as a gift to help pay for my first tattoo. My mother, a tattooed woman herself, said she would pay for the rest. She knew how important this was to me. I felt on top of the world. So a few weeks after my birthday, I headed off for the tattoo parlor with three of my friends. New Tribe, in downtown Toronto, would be the location for my next step toward self-appreciation. For two hours I sat, receiving some of the most amazingly beautiful pain I had ever felt. The tattoo was on my back, a large design of circles, a crop circle to be exact. I had always been fascinated with them, and in high school, ridiculed for believing in something my peers thought to be ridiculous. But I loved them, and I loved my tattoo.

When it was finished and I stood up to look at it in the mirror, I was on the verge of tears. It was gorgeous. My skin was so beautiful. I had never felt like that before. I felt more complete than I had ever felt in my entire life. I was in love with my tattoo and, for the first time, in love with myself. I felt reborn.

When it healed, I took advantage of every chance I had to show it off to the world. It has been almost a year now since my first tattoo, and now, with several more tattoos and another handful of piercings, I feel like an entirely different person than the miserable girl from high school. I am happy with my friends, my life, and with myself.

I owe it to my friends, my university, and most of all, to the simplest of things—a sharp needle, and a little cup of black ink.

Samantha Engbers *is a second-year visual arts major at York University. Born in Victoria, British Columbia, she moved across Canada, finally ending up in Toronto. An abstract artist and a lover of body modification, she hopes to spread awareness about the beauty of body modification through her art.*

The Compass Rose

LUCIE M. WINBORNE

"Oh, my God, no!"

That was my mother's reaction upon learning that her then forty-three-year-old daughter would go under the tattoo needle for the first time. A valid response considering that, as she explained later, "Honey, you'll just have to understand; I was raised in a different generation, and back then, only certain kinds of people got tattoos!"

"Certain kinds of people." Not middle-aged women raised in Christian homes, to be sure.

I'm not sure how old I was when the urge first possessed me to decorate my body with permanent art; somewhere in my late teens, I suppose. Nevertheless, I resisted the desire for three reasons, all of them fear-based. One, fear of the pain; two, fear of changing my mind at a later date and having to endure the allegedly even more painful process of laser removal; and three, the idea of entering a tattoo parlor, which I associated in my mind with the legendary "den of iniquity." As if that weren't enough, how could I ever decide on a design?

A little over two decades later, I was forty-three, nearing my next birthday, and in full midlife crisis mode. The times were not only changing, they were getting late. I had to face the fact that I was never going to magically overcome my fear, but would have to confront it.

In short, I was ready to enter the den of iniquity, populated by who knew what type of characters. I researched the Internet on safety and hygienic issues, asked complete strangers with tattoos about pain thresholds, and enlisted the companionship of a female friend who was, initially, only scheduled to watch (and whose mother-in-law had gotten her first tattoo at age seventy). Only two hurdles remained: finding a design, and finding an artist.

The second task proved easier than I'd expected. A local newspaper magazine profiled a number of area businesses rated "among the best" by their patrons. Trinity Tattoo was highly rated and not far from my house. The first task was a bit more challenging. As a lover of the sea and all things nautical, I was fairly certain that I wanted a nautical design, but the first thing that came to my mind was an anchor, and that was simply too masculine. A ship's wheel? I wasn't a sailor. A fish? I wasn't a fisherman. A ship? Too long. A lighthouse? Too tall. I wanted something small that could be hidden or revealed at will and with ease. I was a white-collar professional, after all, and while

I had no problem with tattoos myself, I wasn't as sure that my current or future employers would feel the same.

I don't know when the words "compass rose" crossed my mind, even though I'd entertained a secret liking for them for years. But somehow I immediately knew—that was it. A compass rose.

Back to the Internet I went. I found various designs, but none of them suited me. They were all so . . . plain. If I was going in for permanent decoration, I wanted something special. And then I found it: A 1607 design from a map by the English topographer John Norden. I didn't know what a topographer was, and I had never heard of John Norden, but something about that simple rose, with its dominant shades of blue and green—the colors of the sea—caught my attention and held it from my first glance. Not wanting to make a hasty decision—this had to be something I could live with into advanced old age, after all—I continued to search for designs. I found a number that I could "live with," but their complexity worried me: more colors, more time, and more pain. And always I came back to John Norden and his sweetly simple work, with its Latin abbreviations of the compass points in beautiful Old English script.

I was caught and nearly held, but still hesitant until, what seemed to be the final confirmation, came at an evening poetry reading. A friend and I sat together and listened to a poet whom neither of us had heard of, but who was obviously quite talented. Then, unexpectedly, he spoke a line about a "girl with a compass rose tattoo on her shoulder." My mouth fell open. My friend's mouth fell open. We looked at each other in disbelief across the table. I knew we were both thinking, *that's it!* It was the sign I was waiting for! I had even already decided that my shoulder would be my chosen location. It was fate.

All that remained was to approach the lion's den—that is, the tattoo parlor. I had sworn for years that I would never have the courage to enter one by myself. Yet that's exactly what I found myself doing when it came time to survey the field, as the friend who had agreed to come as my witness and moral support had another appointment. I'll leave to the reader's imagination what went through my mind when I discovered that Trinity Tattoo's logo was a trinity, all right—of giant skulls!

Nevertheless, I made it inside (where I tried to look as calm and casual as possible) and discovered, to my surprise, that not only was it uninhabited by the Hell's Angels or their ilk, but that it was actually cleaner than my house, with a matter-of-fact and friendly staff. Den of iniquity, indeed! Ward Cleaver wouldn't have minded hanging out there.

A few weeks later, I found myself seated in Trinity's waiting area with my girlfriend (who was now getting her own body ink, at her husband's request), leafing through tattoo magazines while a man who was nearly twice my size moaned, groaned, swore, and finally limped his way through what I learned from his wife was his third inking. This could understandably have deterred any tattoo virgin, but I wasn't backing out now. And when it was my turn, I trembled a bit, breathed a little fast, and—

Endured. I survived! Oh, that first prick wasn't too bad. *Heck, I can handle this*, I thought. And then it got a little more severe, but I stood firm. Tattoo virgin I might be, but I was going to show that 200-plus-pound veteran a thing or two about bravery! Nevertheless, I was grateful for the cool liquid that was applied at regular intervals, as well as the artist's need to "satisfy his nicotine addiction" when we were halfway through.

I was also touched by his regular inquiries as to how I was doing, especially when he called me, near the end of the process, his "little trooper." But most surprising of all was when he asked me the color of my birthstone. "Green," I told him, wondering why on earth he would ask. "Peridot."

"Then I'll put that color in this little diamond in the center," he said. A special touch that, with his gentle shading of the rose's outer golden perimeter, made my nearly 400-year-old design unique.

When I finally saw the finished product, I was both impressed and moved by the artist's skill. True, my shoulder burned like I had a rather bad sunburn, and I had to sleep on my side for several nights afterward (not to mention the obnoxious, healing itch), but I had a true piece of art on my body, one I knew I could indeed live with forever.

When my apprehensive mother saw it, her reaction was one of horror at its size. What I had envisioned as a small design had turned into something almost three times the size, due to the need for more space to insert the Latin lettering. "It looks like a bull's eye!" she exclaimed. Nearly two years later, I don't think she's completely resigned herself to it. Most of all, she was puzzled by my choice of subject. "Why a compass rose?" she asked. "It doesn't really mean anything."

But it does, to me. Unfortunately, explaining that meaning to anyone else has so far eluded me, except for in vague terms. The closest I've been able to come was in the closing lines of a poem I wrote about the experience:

Yet I rarely look as deeply
at the question why a compass
Except sometimes to wonder

if Norden would smile
at this use of his rose
Or if reading the chart
of an unmapped life
would nod the secret comfort
in its heading of true north.

Its heading of true north. That is, I think, what really spoke to me in the end. A silent pointer to guide one in the right direction on a steady course. A spiritual meaning known only to me, in the colors of the sea that I love.

Lucie M. Winborne *is an executive assistant at Ripley Entertainment, Inc., in Orlando, Florida. In her free time she enjoys reading, writing poetry and fiction, and her cat, Chloe.*

It's a Wonderful Life

JEAN M. MILLER

A tattoo? Me? I would never get one of those nasty things!

That is what I would have said twenty years ago if you had asked me. When I was a young adult in the 1980s, I thought that the only people who had tattoos were motorcycle guys and people who had been to prison. I would have never even envisioned myself with a tattoo anywhere! Isn't it funny how you get fat on the words you eat?

I had been going through a really rough patch in my life. With the loss of my mother—my best friend—to breast cancer, and realizing that my forty-two-year-old self was aging quickly, I felt the need to make some drastic changes.

Famous *Inked Chicks*

Mick Beasley has been an advocate and activist for the promotion of safe tattooing for over twenty years. She's a tattoo artist herself and co-owns Dragon Moon Studio in Glen Burnie, Maryland, with her husband Tom. Mick's list of accomplishments, including founding the Alliance of Professional Tattooists (APT) in 1992, is so extensive it can't all be listed here. To that end, the National Tattoo Association established a new award in her honor—Outstanding Contributions to the Tattoo Profession—which she received in 1994.

I knew that I needed to take better care of myself physically, as this is something my mother—wonderful, kind, and talented though she may have been—did not do. I wasn't in terrible shape, but I could do better. I decided that I wanted to participate in the next Susan G. Komen Race for a Cure, so I started walking more, running a little, and bought myself an elliptical machine.

In the middle of all of this, I felt a sense of renewal. I was working out more. I was listening to music again; something I had gotten away from over the years. I was dressing snazzier and taking more care with my makeup. I let my short, spiky hair grow out again and went back to my original color. And then one day, while at a family gathering, my twenty-one-year-old niece was talking about her tattoos and body piercings (she had quite a few). The rest of the family is somewhat critical of her, but I was intrigued. I wasn't crazy about the piercings, but I loved her tattoos. That was when the seed was planted.

When I brought up the subject of tattoos to one of my "hip" friends at work—who happens to be twelve years older than me—she told me that she thought tattoos were great and had always wanted one herself. That was all I needed to validate myself; I wanted a tattoo!

Oddly enough, I work in a medium-security men's prison as a substance abuse counselor. Trust me, I have seen more than my fair share of tattoos. Some were gorgeous, some were rough, and some were just plain crazy. (Some of them were in places I couldn't see—thank goodness!) I had heard a lot about them, but didn't know exactly how it all worked. I talked to some friends, searched the Internet, and finally decided what I wanted—something on my lower back. I thought a tattoo peeking out above the waistband was very sexy, and yes, I could still be sexy at forty-two.

So I made the appointment and e-mailed a friend to ask if she would go with me. She agreed to go, but firmly stated that she was not getting one. However, she would be glad to watch me be in pain—what a gal. We had been friends for thirty years, so I forgave her for that one. We made our arrangements to meet.

I was so excited that morning I could hardly stand it. I met my gal pal and traveled to Owensboro, Kentucky, for the big appointment. While we were driving there, my husband called me to tell me that he was upset that I was getting a tattoo. I politely asked him if he was insane. I wanted to know what the problem was, as he had known for weeks that I wanted to do this. He said he just didn't know if he'd like it. Men! He wasn't worried about my pain or my safety—just whether or not he was going to like it. I assured him that I was not getting a skull and crossbones across my back, promised he would love it, and hung up on him. Unfortunately, that really put a damper on my pre-tattoo excitement buzz. My friend decided to stop for a couple of pick-me-up margaritas, which weren't very good, but helped me feel better, and soon we were back on track.

Once there, the tattoo artists at Shadow of Illusion helped me finalize my design. Howell and Ashley were helpful in getting my idea on paper. It was time. As my heart raced and my dear friend observed, I got my lovely tattoo. It's on my lower back, just under my back surgery battle scar from eleven years ago. There's a large, purple flower in the center with black vines and green leaves branching outward. Then, there is a pink flower on each of the vines, to honor my late mother and father. It hurt, but it was a good pain. When I looked at it for the first time, I couldn't believe I had done it, but I was so glad I had. It was awesome. My pal, Donna, was speechless, but was eventually able to declare that she loved it. We left to continue our girls' day out, to do some shopping and have lunch.

Reactions? Most people love it. My seven-year-old son thinks I am very cool. A friend's husband told me that it is the tackiest thing he's ever seen—and he loves it. My own husband didn't really care for my tattoo at first, but it has grown on him. He even finds it a little sexy now! But what is most important is that I love it. It is a symbol of my losses, my loves, and my future. It is me.

That's not the end of the story, though. A month after I got my lovely back tattoo, I started giving thought to yet one more. I have been told they are addictive, and it is so true. So I recently got a very cool pink flower on my toe. It, too, is beautiful—I can't stop looking at it. My husband fears that I will come home with my arms sleeved or something. Almost everyone else thinks it's as cool as I do.

At forty-two, I finally feel free to do things because I want to and not be concerned by what someone else may think. That is the most liberating feeling. I read a passage the other day by Frances Lear that summed it up pretty well. "I believe the second half of one's life is meant to be better than the first half. The first half is finding out how you do it. And the second half is enjoying it."

Enjoy *your* life.

Jean M. Miller is a proud soccer, judo, and basketball mom to her seven-year-old son, Tony, who is her joy. She has been married to her husband Paul for twelve years, has a bachelor's degree in social work, and enjoys many hobbies such as antiques, shopping, and flower gardening.

A Small Price to Pay

MELODY BARBOSA

My tattoos have caused a stir with a few of my family members. My mother's family is quite conservative about them, partially due to religious beliefs. I was raised in the Jewish faith, and learned early on that Jews are forbidden to be tattooed. This restriction excludes tattooed Jews from receiving a Jewish burial. For this reason, I have been scolded many times by my maternal grandmother for getting tattooed.

On the paternal side of my family, my grandmother thought my tattoo was great. I'm not sure if she was just humoring me, but I was appreciative just the same. My parents, whom I consider to be pretty open-minded, don't really like them, but try to be accepting of me. My mom is generally supportive, but tells me not to be pushy about the subject. My dad sees tattoos as negative and warns me that I may be associated with a 'bad element" by having them.

My grandfather was the first person to have an influence on my tattooed future. He would sit in his easy chair and entertain me with stories of his days in the navy, about his fellow sailors and their tattoos. No, my grandfather didn't have any himself, but his stories were enough to provide my young mind with fuel for my future passion. The one story that always comes to mind is that of bawdy, WWII sailors competing—through various layers of undress—to prove that they had more tattoos than the next guy. Before I had even see tattoo art, I had images floating through my mind of traditional sailor tattoos on flexed chests and women that could dance on arms. This first exposure to tattoos could have amounted to nothing, but instead it started me off with a positive and flamboyant view of the art that I would come to love and eventually pursue as a profession. My grandfather's sailor stories were the only exposure I had, early on, to tattoos and tattooing. Since I had never heard anyone else discuss the subject, I'm pretty sure that I'm the only one in my family with tattoos.

At the age of thirteen, as I was coming into my own, I decided, *I want to get a tattoo!* I already had three piercings in each ear and felt ready to move to the next level, which for me was a tattoo. I don't recall exactly what, at thirteen, I was so fascinated with in regard to tattoos. I just remember seeing other people with them and wanting them for myself. I knew full well that tattoos were permanent and that I would carry them with me for the rest of my life. I didn't mention wanting to get a tattoo, but started to think of a design that would best represent me.

The tattoo idea simmered for a while, and in high school I found myself exchanging hand-poked tattoos with a friend. I had no problem with getting the ink in deep enough to stay, but she found the sound of the needle poking through the skin disturbing. Years later, I wear no evidence of this first tattooing endeavor, but she will always have my tattoo as a memory of that day.

At age nineteen, I felt that I had finally hit on the symbolism that best represented me at the time. A lotus, which grows in the mud of a pond and blooms beautifully above the water, mirrored the transition I was feeling at that time in my life.

I was so excited to get my first tattoo, but nervous, too. I didn't know what to expect. I didn't think much about the pain; at the time, I was more concerned with having to lower my pants for some stranger to tattoo me. I tried to talk to the tattoo artist while he was working, which was a big no-no. I later learned, while giving my first machine tattoo, that it's not really a good idea to distract the artist at work.

I was so excited about the whole experience that I tried to memorize everything that happened. In the end, the tattoo didn't really hurt, but the pain wouldn't have mattered much to me, anyway. The experience of getting my first tattoo was completely mine. I feel more connected to it because I drew the design and paid for it myself. The process of getting the tattoo had changed me for the better, and I felt like a new person, stronger and more independent. The first tattoo turned out to be just the tip of the iceberg for me. I soon wanted more of them, so I educated myself on anything and everything related to tattoo art, history, and culture. In my quest for tattoo information, I found that I not only wanted to *get* tattoos, but *give* them as well. It was probably the hand-poked tattoo that I gave my future husband that sealed the idea of being a tattoo artist. Since that day, he has continued to be a willing participant in my artistic advancement, even being my first machine tattoo "victim."

When I got around to my second tattoo, I had already begun apprenticing in a shop in Hawaii. My mentor drew up a design for me and I picked the spot—the inside of my left arm. After the first tattoo, I wanted all of them to be symbolic of my life in some way. I also wanted all of them to be original art. I told him the elements I wanted in the tattoo—skulls and stars with a traditional feel—and he worked up a design for me. The skull ended up with a pirate patch and an ornate dagger through it. As a nod to my future children, he included a fetus in the handle of the dagger. To top off the design, he added a swirl of stars circling around the skull and dagger. Thankfully, this design was just what I as looking for and broke me out of the symbolic mindset. By getting this one on the inside of my arm, I quickly learned that not every tattoo location feels the same. Before the tattoo was started, I was warned about the pain in that particular area, but I figured it would look cool there and the pain wouldn't last forever. Thanks to the skill of the artist, it was over rather quickly, although it did seem longer to me. But the pain didn't deter me—even though it hurt, I want to get another tattoo on the other side. The tattoo itself may have been just for fun, but it serves as a memory of my time in Hawaii and the beginning of my apprenticeship. I often find myself looking at my tattoos and enjoy getting compliments on them.

I am still working on my apprenticeship, and it seems that it has helped me learn a lot about myself as well as tattooing.

Tattoos are very personal—sometimes a life-changing experience—and it's fascinating that by being the artist, I get to be included in this intimate part of someone's life.

I still try to be considerate of my family's feelings, but choose not to hide my tattoos. They are a source of pride for me and despite all of my family's reactions and feedback, good or bad, I will go on collecting my tattoos. In the meantime I will cover up for synagogue and keep my tattoo enthusiasm to myself around them. Discretion is a small price to pay to maintain my individuality.

Melody Barbosa is twenty-five years old and lives in Maryland with her husband, whom she eloped with in Las Vegas—Elvis style—fulfilling a lifelong dream. She's continuing her studies as an apprentice tattoo artist and looks forward to enjoying professional status.

Jie Mei

LIZ ENTMAN

I'm reclining on a padded table in a cool, sterile
room, with my jeans and underwear yanked
down to my pubic bone and the hem of my
sweater pulled up to my rib cage. Someone is
playing Hank Williams down the hall. I try not
to shiver as my belly is shaved of its fine blond
down and a purple design is transferred to my
skin. There's a snap of new latex, a chilly spritz
of disinfectant, and a swipe of clear, cool jelly.

"Ready?" Ian asks.

"Yep," I say. I try to sound cavalier. I suddenly
realize that I've met Ian once before, about
four years ago. He pierced my navel when I was
sixteen and he was an apprentice. My navel
is showing now, but he doesn't recognize his
work, or me.

Of course, back then I wore a lot of black and metal, and today I'm wearing a lavender sweater from the Gap, so there's a contextual gulf he'd have to overcome to connect the dots. I don't even live here anymore—I've been away at college for the last year and a half. I decide not to reintroduce myself.

Ian sits on the swiveling stool beside my hip. He steps on a pedal and the tattoo machine begins to emit a stern, familiar hum.

I love this sound. It reminds me of a fetal heartbeat on an ultrasound scanner, like the moment where what you love meets what you see.

"Okay?" Ian confirms. He's resting the side of his hand on my hipbone, the needle surging in the air above my stomach, pulsing like a thousand adrenaline-charged butterflies.

"Go for it," I say.

I watch him tilt his hand, touch the needle to my body, and begin to stitch black pigment deep into the dermal cells of my skin. I'm so startled by the pain, I actually gasp. I have two other tattoos on my back, but this is way more intense. I'm not sure if I want to look, but I do anyway.

Watching Ian draw my blood infuses the pain with a new, weird kind of intimacy, and I realize that I actually prefer it this way. I once dated a man with a pain fetish. He had full sleeves tattooed on his arms, and thirteen holes in his body that he hadn't been born with. He had observed every modification intently, even when he had a fourteen-gauge needle driven through his privates. It had made no sense at the time, but now I have a sudden flash of insight.

I realize that much of what makes pain so painful is just the surprise and the fear that accompany it. If you walk into a plate-glass door that you didn't know was there, you're going to cry as much from being startled as you will for your wounds. But make the pain voluntary, seek it out and give it a purpose, and you're somehow better armed against the next black eye or broken heart life throws at you.

The revelation is intoxicating. I want to laugh. Adrenaline is surging up and down my spine, flushing my earlobes and curling my fingers, rendering my breath rapid and shallow, my irises quivering at the sight of my own blood and, for a brief moment, I see how my ex could confuse this for lust.

It's my sister's eighteenth birthday, and this tattoo is my present to her. It means "big sister" in Cantonese. We have no connection to China besides Christmas dinners at the Golden Dragon restaurant, but we like how the characters, put together, look like an ancient ritual mask. If all the world's a stage, sisterhood is my breakout role.

Besides the fact that she is my only sibling, my first memory is of the day my parents brought her home from the hospital. So this is also the eighteenth anniversary of the beginning of my own remembered life.

My sister isn't actually here for this, however. We've switched places for the week: I am back in town for the holidays, but she has gone to visit her boyfriend, who coincidentally goes to college in the same city I do. Right now, some guy is quilting a pair of masklike Cantonese letters meaning "little sister" into the lower left quadrant of her belly. The location is a mirror image of mine; if we hugged, the tattoos would touch.

But we don't do a lot of hugging lately. We're like matter and antimatter—we can barely be in the same room together.

It wasn't always like this, though. I believe in second chances, and—I wasn't sure until I proposed this tattoo idea—so does she.

We knew something was wrong early on, even when she was three. She's had cycles of psychotic depression and mania. She's a pathological liar. She used to burn herself with cigarettes and once carved runic symbols into her chest, thinking it might protect her from the nagging voices that drove her obsessions. She pulled out all her hair and ate it. And that was when she was *on* her medication.

Our realities rarely intersected, but we made up for it in loyalty. I stood up for her at school, I pinned flowers into her hair to hide the bald spots, covered her lies, and kept her secrets. In return she trusted and listened to me.

But two years ago, when she was sixteen and I was almost eighteen, she had another spell of psychotic depression and became convinced that there was not enough love in the world for both of us. It was as if her mind had suddenly become allergic to me; sibling rivalry ate at her in ways I could never imagine.

Famous *Inked Chicks*

Betty Broadbent has a rather extensive list of credentials. In 1972, at age seventeen, she joined the Ringling Brothers Circus and quickly became labeled as "one of America's most loved, most photographed, tattooed women." She was also accredited with being the "youngest tattooed woman in the world." Her desire for independence caused Betty to seek out sideshow attention and the subsequent paychecks. She even entered herself in the 1939 World's Fair televised beauty contest, not with a focus on winning, but to garnish the benefits of the free publicity.

It was a traitorous plate-glass door that had descended unnoticed between us, and when we crashed into it, we instinctively recoiled from each other and stared at our cuts in anger, betrayal, and disbelief.

Our parents, with toxic naiveté, refused to acknowledge the fact that I made her sicker, and that her sickness made her as abusive toward me as she was toward herself. They would not hospitalize her or let me move out. Neither one of us could take it. Six months later, I accepted admission into the first out-of-state college that would take me.

Ian pauses to change needles. "Looks good so far," he says brightly, if someone with such an uncanny resemblance to Kurt Cobain could ever be described as bright. "Hurt much?"

"It's not so bad," I say. Now that he's using a shading tip to fill in the outline, there's a lot more blood. I suppose I haven't really shed more than a tablespoon, but it's awfully red against the paper towels.

Since I left, my sister's gotten her GED and has enrolled at a local community college. She has long hair again. She works part-time. She's got a boyfriend. But she still unhinges a little when I come back to visit, starts pulling out her hair again and picking fights—bad ones. I'm not surprised she left as soon as I came to town. I would have stayed away, but I was too homesick.

It occurs to me that this can't be my home anymore, that I'm making my skin my home and am furnishing it appropriately. A bird, for flight. A flower, for my roots. And this bonding through ink that is supposed to somehow make up for the fact that we can't bridge the necessary distance that keeps her disease from achieving critical mass.

But it's not so much an act of compensation as it is one of faith, or maybe just insurance. Her birth is my first memory; I can't untangle my identity as an individual from my identity as her sister. I want this fact recorded somewhere I can't lose it, no matter where I go next.

Ian wipes away the last of the blood and ink, slathers my new scar with a milky smear of bacitracin, and covers it with a bandage. I touch it gently; it's tender, a little swollen, and it's the most beautiful thing in the world.

My sister and I will probably pass each other on the interstate tomorrow. We won't agree to meet halfway to share a cup of coffee or anything. Our tattoos will itch against our seatbelts, but we'll just light cigarettes and drive on past each other, waiting for the new skin to grow.

Liz Entman lives in Brooklyn, New York. She writes and makes money correcting other people's grammar. She's currently planning to move to the middle of nowhere to finish a book. Her sister is living a happy, independent life back home. She calls sometimes.

Pawprints on My Heart

CHARLOTTE BREWSTER

I love tattoos because they are visual stories, and writers love stories. I especially love it when someone's ink makes you stop and think.

I have either two tattoos or fourteen, depending on your perspective. My first one is a Celtic knot work heart inside a star. To me, the tangled heart represents how complicated love can be—with the reminder that love is in the details—and yet, somehow it all works out. The star it sits upon is a powerful symbol of the vulnerability that's necessary to truly give and receive love. A star is like an open hand.

While my first tattoo represents my personal theory of love, my second memorializes love in practice. This tattoo, or collection of tattoos, is an unlikely love story: two strays, one friendship. On February 28, 2004, one of my best friends died. She was twenty-seven-years old. She also happened to be a feline. She was a tiny, runty stray with uncommonly muted calico colors of peach, gray, and white instead of the usual black and orange. She appeared in my life when I was just five years old—the same year my parents got divorced, I realized my dad was a "bad guy," and childhood got a lot harder. I opened the front door, and there she was walking up our front lawn toward me as if to say, "Yep, this is the place. I'm home." I picked her up, and that was it; she'd found her human. I named her Bright Eyes, but, being five, I would pet her and coo, "wooja, wooja, wooja," so we ended up just calling her Wooja.

Wooja lived an amazing twenty-seven years with me. One night in late 2002, quite suddenly, Wooja experienced a jolting seizure, and I raced her to the emergency vet. Thus began one of the hardest years of my adulthood. I was referred to the acclaimed Davis facility, where she underwent a series of tests. Although her condition was considered neurological in nature, it could not be pinpointed without continued stress to Wooja. It could have been a tumor. It could have been a disease. I'll never know. When I was first allowed to see her after the tests, she was so weak and small. I sang "You Are My Sunshine" to her and sobbed as she ate a little food for me. The trip home was excruciating as I begged the universe for no traffic—that we just make it home—during the long drive, while she, my copilot in childhood, rested weakly on the passenger seat.

Once she stabilized from her medications and daily fluids, I purchased a nontoxic inkpad and "booked" her paw, a replica to take to the tattoo artist. To honor our time together, I had her paw tattooed four times up my left calf. Wooja soldiered on for about another year. I stayed home as much as possible and nursed her through her sad transition. Even thinking about this period of time—how my mom would drive up to sit with her so I could bartend and make a little extra money for her costly meds, the stress of never knowing when another seizure would hit, the pain of holding and talking her through a spell, the sad but tender goodbyes, and her cute way of sleeping with her face in my hand—brings tears to my eyes even now.

After she passed, I sank into a deep depression that I later sought therapy to ease. There were literally days where I moved from the bed to the couch and then back to the bed; I felt halved. I didn't have the mindset of an adult woman. I was grieving for her as the five-year-old child who found her would. It was as if I had to mourn in the appropriate stage for each decade we'd been together: the tomboy years when we both spent much of our time climbing trees, the adolescent years when she spent much time licking tears off my face, the searching twenties when she tolerated my numerous forays to the outside world with the confidence that she'd always be with me, and the beginning of my hard-won thirties, when I finally began to hold my head up high and be the woman I'd always wanted to be—the woman our unique bond had helped me become.

In March of 2006, I had the original four paw prints darkened and nine more added, so that they extend up my whole left leg for a total of lucky thirteen. They weave their way up as if she'd trudged through some ink and then right up my leg—and into my sad but still open heart.

Sasha Merritt was the perfect artist for this profound experience. She was extremely thoughtful and receptive to the story, and she mentioned how much she loved doing memorial tattoos, especially those for beloved pets. She also encouraged me to bring pictures in on the day, so that Wooja was there in image as well as spirit.

I love it when people notice the paws because it gives me the chance to talk about Wooja's remarkable life. When I'm wearing hosiery, people often ask if the paw prints are painted on the nylons or tattoos. I love telling folks that they're "real" and the story of the special kitty's paws they represent. Just the other day, the paw prints stopped traffic as I was running!

Recently, the paw prints have taken on an added meaning as I've been training to run my first ever half marathon. When I catch a glimpse of the paw prints as I run, I feel an extra little boost, like she is there with me, urging me to live my life as fully as I can, to go a little farther, push a little harder, and accomplish a little more. I don't expect everyone to understand, but if you've been lucky enough to be uniquely bonded to a pet, then you know how you feel isn't—and doesn't have to be—"grown up." It's an instinctive reaction: the strong emotions you can only experience in childhood—because you're feeling them for the first time. Even the memory of them is palpable.

I believe that pets often purvey (or is that "purr"vey?) the unconditional love our souls seek. Wooja gave me that when my world seemed bleak and bizarre compared to how other kids' lives seemed. I often say that she was sent to me to make my life bearable. She did, and she still does to this day.

Letting any kind of love into your life and heart means signing a contract for delayed grief; you get years of comfort and heartbreakingly beautiful memories, but the bill at the end is painfully difficult to pay. Somehow, though, it is always worth it, every time. Wooja's little paw print tattoos remind me of how far I have come as a woman, how friendship in any form can save you, and that she is always with me: paw-printed on my leg, imprinted on my spirit, and curled up in my heart.

Charlotte Brewster is a writer, though she calls herself an inkbot, enjoying the dual reference to writing and tattoos. Charlotte resides in "the glorified hallway" in San Francisco with her lovable, if ironically spazzy, cat named Zen.

My Life as a Suit

TARA GODDARD

My tattoos are not, for the most part, a sign of rebellion. They do not mark me as some wild radical living life on the edge. They do not tell stories of a seedy underworld life, nor do they hint at some edgy, exciting person hidden beneath. But even though I don't fit those old-fashioned stereotypes of the inked person, I admit I do get a kick out of surprising people with them, even after years of being tattooed. The surprise is most drastic for people who meet me in the professional setting with its attendant dress codes.

The business suit, like the tattoo suit, immediately leads people to certain assumptions. And the business suit, like the tattoo suit, can have either positive or negative connotations in the eye of the beholder. To some, a business suit gives the immediate impression of competence, of professional confidence and power, of the wearer as a "mover and shaker." Yet, to others, a business suit is reminiscent of corporate greed, corruption, and rigidly conservative attitudes. Similarly, the tattoo suit can be viewed from opposite ends of the spectrum. To some, the tattoo suit is the garb of a criminal personality, a shady personage, a crazed and possibly dangerous person. Yet, to others, a tattoo suit is the sign of ultimate devotion to the art form, a sign of dedication and the ultimate passage through trials of time, pain (or at least intense discomfort), and money. It speaks to an intimate relationship with an artist, and a commitment on both physical and emotional levels.

Yet, as common as tattoos have become—particularly in the middle and upper-middle class—the tattoo suit and the business suit are seen as conflicting images, or not conceived together at all. Partly, this is the nature of the business suit. As the metaphorical armor of the business world, it provides full coverage of whatever lies beneath, be it inked skin or bare. And despite today's increasing acceptance of tattoos, the business world is one of the last strongholds of antiquated conceptions of "acceptable" and "normal." So the business suit can override the tattooed suit by its mere presence.

This conflict between the business suit and tattoos became real for me when I started my first true "power suit" job. It was October, and the weather was already cool enough to necessitate wearing pants and long sleeves. Additionally, since I was new to the job, I was unclear how much, if any, visible ink would be permissible. So I erred on the side of caution and kept all tattoos covered with professional pantsuits or dressy slacks. In addition to looking "professional" in the workplace, the business suit was an outward sign of my inward excitement about leaping into new territory: the high-powered government world. For me, covering up had nothing to do with being ashamed or fearing pubic disapproval of my tattoos—rather, it was a sign of upward movement and growth.

Over the next few months, I earned a reputation as being a reliable, hardworking employee (I was actually a Fellow, so I was simultaneously a grunt and a go-to person). I grew into my business suit as I grew into myself, gaining increased confidence and comfort mixing with high-level politicians and government employees. In addition, in my small office, I built comfortable, fun relationships with my coworkers and supervisors. They learned of my rather benign hobbies of reading, crafting, and volunteering. During this time, my coworkers thus developed certain expectations of my dress, my manner, and my interests.

After seven months on the job, the weather began to warm quickly. With increasing temperatures and Casual Fridays came knee-length skirts, sleeveless blouses, and generally increased amounts of visible skin. I felt comfortable in my place in the office, and on one Casual Friday I wore a crisp set of capris, a nice blouse, and dress shoes. These short pants bared the dragons that flow on each leg from toes to knees. On the left, an earth- and water-themed dragon grins, his leaf-shaped wings wrapping around the back of my calf, his tail changing into a large wave curling across the top of my foot. On the other side, a wise crone dragon is wreathed with a mane of cloud-inspired curls, her tail sweeping into flames across the top of my right foot. Both dragons are kind and reflect reverence for nature and fantasy, as befits my interests and personality, but as far as everyone else was concerned, they are still dragons. Tattooed dragons. To say that jaws dropped and eyebrows raised would be an understatement.

It was interesting to watch the internal conflict of my closest coworkers, evidenced by their facial expressions and initially cautious, increasingly probing questions (the usual "Why," "Did it hurt," "What did your mother say" type of questions). On one hand, I had long proven myself to fit something of a "normal" mold in their eyes. Additionally, I had proven myself to be competent, intelligent, and decidedly nonthreatening. Yet, the sudden appearance of an expanse of ink evoked conscious and subconscious stereotypes of a less endearing sort.

However, due to their open natures and our developed relationships, people quickly grew accepting (if not approving) of my artwork. I am not glossing over or flashing forward—people truly took the ink in stride more quickly than I would have guessed. I do admit that it was a calculated risk on my part—I felt comfortable in both my role in the office and my relationship with my coworkers to bare my ink and consequently, their possible preconceived notions.

I did not realize, however, just how much these coworkers appreciated my tattoos, or at least appreciated what a large part of me that they are. My fellowship ended in the office after one year and I prepared to return to graduate school. My coworkers decided to throw me a party and take me out to lunch. I was instructed to meet them at the restaurant at the predetermined time. Beforehand, there were some whispered conferences that halted abruptly at my approach, but I figured it was the usual party planning—maybe a cake would appear at the end of lunch, accompanied by an embarrassing serenade by the restaurant employees.

When I met my coworkers and we sat down for lunch, there was an expectant silence, broken by some giggles from my coworkers. All of a sudden, they began to remove long-sleeved sweaters or push up their sleeves. Everyone at the party had applied fake tattoos on their arms, chests, or hands. I stared around in amazement—here were my coworkers, all business-suit wearers themselves, some of them the same generation as my parents, plastered with various fake tattoos as a joke and sign of fondness for me. I admit I got a bit teary-eyed. That was one of the nicest things anyone has ever done for me.

I think we all learned a lesson from the appearance of my dragons in the office. Many of them were forced to replace old notions with a new paradigm because of a tattooed friend. Conversations sparked by my tattoos allowed me to educate people on the level to which the art form has been raised in the last two decades, and to the many reasons that people choose to get inked. And with their tattooed sendoff, they taught me that people can be even more accepting than I could hope, and quicker to appreciate my good qualities than "fault" me for choices with which they might not immediately (or ever) identify.

Tara Goddard (also known as InkedBuddha) started drawing on herself with colored markers at an early age, and to her parent's dismay, she never grew tired of wearing ink on her skin. She is a devoted tattoo enthusiast, based in Sacramento, California, and has spent countless hours on the Internet looking at tattoo designs.

Just One of the Guys

BABETTE LANE JINKINS

When I walk up to the counter to greet the clients that just walked in the door of our tattoo shop, I often hear the question, "Are the guys who do the tattoos here?" I answer with my standard response, "Yes, the artists are here." I know what's coming next—it's always the same. "Could you go get one, so that I can talk directly to him about what I want done?"

This is where I get to have fun. I ask them what they're wanting, and wait for the response. Sometimes I get one, but sometimes I just get confused stares, ignored, or told to go get the artist. Then I smile and politely inform them that they are talking to one of the "guys," and hand them my portfolio.

I'll give them a few minutes, and then ask if I can help them. Most of the time, I get to hear an apology. I have had others tell me flat out that they would not let a woman touch them, since women "can't tattoo."

I wish I could say that this prejudice started with the clients. Unfortunately, it started long before that. When I was a child, I remember going with my dad while he was being tattooed. I mentioned then that I was interested in learning. While my dad supported the idea from the time I first brought it up, it seemed that everyone else thought it was humorous and would politely suggest alternate career choices.

It didn't end there. When I met my husband, who is a tattoo artist, and began helping around the studio, I approached him about learning how to tattoo. By this time, I was in my mid-twenties and hoped that attitudes would have changed. Imagine my shock when I heard my future husband tell me, "I

Famous *Inked Chicks*

Pat Fish began tattooing in 1984, just a few years before the boom in tattoo popularity. She is most widely known for her tattoo specialty—Celtic knot work—which is one of the favorite styles among collectors, and there aren't many artists that specialize in it. Pat's Irish heritage sparked her interest to combine two of her loves into one, and she's been named "the Celtic Queen of the West Coast." Pat has received much recognition for her work despite the fact that she doesn't attend many conventions (due to her latex allergy). Pat tattoos at her studio, Tattoo Santa Barbara, in California.

will never teach a woman to tattoo. I've said that for years—the only one I would consider teaching is my daughter, and she's not interested anymore."

I dropped the subject for a while and continued helping in the studio by answering phones, doing paperwork, sterilizing equipment; whatever grunt work needed to be done, I did it. I began an apprenticeship to learn body piercing and, after a few years, went above and beyond my teacher. I dedicated a lot of time to learning anything and everything I could about piercing, during which I made it a point to watch him tattoo and ask as many questions as I could. About every four to six months, I would propose the idea to him again, and still be told no.

In the meantime, I was learning how to make needles and doing the line drawings for him, on top of the rest of the duties I was performing in the studio. After about four years of this, I was fed up. I again approached my husband, and asked the redundant question. I had already told myself this would be the last time I would ask about an apprenticeship. If I was told no, he could return to making his own needles and doing his own sterilizing. I think something in my face, or the way I asked, let him know that I was at the end of my rope.

He asked me why. I told him, again, about how I wanted it since I was a young child and that it was another way that I could grow artistically. I guess my answer was right, as I was then handed a tattoo machine, told to learn how to tear it down completely and that it had better work as good, if not better, after I put it back together. Little did I know that this was only the beginning of an intense course of basic training, tattoo style.

Not only was I not allowed to trace line drawings for him (they had to be freehanded), but I also had to sit with him for any and every tattoo that came in when I had free time. I set up his workstation before he would do the tattoos, and then tore it down and cleaned it afterward. It was another three months before I was allowed to do anything but hold a running tattoo machine. My first clients were honeydew melons. Real skin was still a long ways off.

As I read back through what I've written so far, it doesn't sound so bad, but I realize that I left out a lot of details. A lot of people will wonder how it was so difficult. Let me start by saying that anytime I complained about a new task, or stood up for what I thought I should be allowed to do, I was told very firmly that I didn't have any idea what I was talking about. And then I would be expected to go home with this man—the same one that had made me angry enough to see red—and revert back to my role as wife with no hard feelings or mention of what went on not thirty minutes earlier at work.

The first time I was told I could touch skin, I was so excited, I was beside myself. Then, the nervousness set in. This happened every time I was allowed to practice—I practiced on myself and my friends. Looking back, I don't know why some of them let me do it, and I owe them all a big "thank you." If it weren't for them, I wouldn't be where I am today.

I also have to hand it to my husband, as much as I hated him through some of it; I'm glad he put me through what he did. I also see now that through those first few years, when I kept asking for an apprenticeship, I already had one.

I have talked to other artists that have the same amount of time in as I do, and most of them don't know how to make their own needles, let alone any other secrets of the trade. Most of them also did apprenticeships, but are just now learning some of the most basic things. They may have more skin time in, but

I have them beat hands down on the details. But I'm still learning, too, and don't plan to ever stop. I feel that the day I stop learning is the day I need to lay my machine down for good.

I still smile when I greet the clients or answer the phone and hear, "I want to talk to the guys that do the tattoos." It used to upset me, but now it's a way to show them that the "standard" isn't so standard after all. I've now been doing it long enough that the word is out that a woman works here, and now I get clients asking for me by name. I know that I'll never be completely accepted by every single client, and that's okay with me. For every one that can't accept me, there's another client that just wants an artist and doesn't care whether the tattooist is a man or a woman, as long as he or she can lay down a clean piece of work. That's me—just one of the guys.

Babette Lane Jinkins was born a small-town Kansas girl in 1975, but moved to Dumas, Texas, where she met her mentor and husband, Shanty. Together, they own and operate Texas Inkslingers in Dumas. Babette has three children, ages six, nine, and twelve.

Future Tattooed Women of the World, Unite!

AMY BROZIO-ANDREWS

Though she's only four, I suspect my daughter will be coming home with a tattoo as soon as she is legally able to do so without needing a parent's permission. She was first introduced to tattoos about eighteen months ago. Emma loves getting mail, and my mother often includes stickers in the cards she sends her grandchildren. When Emma was almost three, my mother sent her a St. Patrick's Day card with temporary tattoos—green, glittery Celtic patterns and shamrocks.

At first, Emma thought they were stickers, sighing with frustration that she couldn't get them to stick to anything. Again and again, she'd press them onto the wall or her hand only to watch them flutter to the floor. When I saw what she was trying to do, I explained to her that these were tattoos—a special kind of sticker for your skin that stays on for a long, long time, even through a bath. She was skeptical ("Pictures that stick to my arm? Even through a bath?") but eager and willing to give it a try. She jumped up and down in anticipation, brown curls bouncing, as I snipped out a small shamrock from the sheet of designs with sharp kitchen scissors, removed the plastic film from the paper backing, and wet a washcloth to apply it to her skin.

I stood her up on the closed toilet seat in the bathroom. Emma looked at me funny and began to squirm when I placed the tattoo on her skin and held it there with the washcloth, coaching her to stand still for just thirty seconds. I put it on her tummy, upside down so it would be right side up when she lifted her shirt to look at it. As soon as I took the washcloth away, she brushed her fingers over the image of the tiny green three-leafed clover. Alarmed by the permanence of it, she immediately began shrieking at me to "get it off!" like I'd just applied acid to her skin. So out came the bottle of baby oil and I scrubbed off her first tattoo about ten seconds after she got it, thinking nothing of it, except that at least she got a taste of something fun. I'd just put the tattoos away and maybe during the summer she'd be interested in trying again.

Oh, she got a taste, all right. About twenty minutes later, she decided she wanted to wear the Celtic bracelet tattoo around her little wrist after all, permanence be damned.

That temporary tattoo bracelet must have lasted almost a month. After every meal, I'd wash her hands and face and she'd warn, "Be careful of my tattoo!" She'd check it carefully after

Famous *Inked Chicks*

SuzAnne Fauser struggled to earn her place in the tattoo industry, though she technically began tattooing in 1979, feeling that male artists attempted to deter her from progress because they were threatened by her and female artists in general. She served a useless apprenticeship, under a man whose name she refused to reveal (as an act of revenge, she admitted), and resorted to tactics of flattery in order to garner information from male tattoo artists. Then she met Paul Rogers, who taught her many of the technical aspects of tattooing, and she became a sensation. SuzAnne passed away in 2001.

every bath, making sure it was intact, noting every little deterioration of the design as time went on. She showed it to all her friends, her grandparents, the cashier on the checkout line at the grocery store. Emma absolutely beamed with pride at her tattoo.

Once it was finally lost to the soap and water of the tub, Emma began needling me for another, like a little temporary tattoo junkie. "Can I have another tattoo today, Mommy? Please? I'll go turn on the faucet and get a washcloth. You go get the scissors."

Neither my husband nor I have any tattoos, but ever since then, she's been fascinated by my brothers' tattoos—their angular designs, skulls, and monsters—so dark and so different than the bright and colorful shamrocks, hearts, and fairies she wears. She looks at their tattoos intently and my brothers allow Emma to touch them gingerly with her little fingers. I think she's still working out exactly what real tattoos are. I haven't told her yet that real tattoos are applied with ink and needles, and that it probably hurts—God forbid she tries to give herself one with a sewing needle and a Magic Marker. (Hey, say what you will, but I know my child; other kids may have an independent streak a mile wide, but my kid's is deeper than the Mariana Trench.)

Last summer, when her Uncle Craig decided to have some fun with Emma, he told her that tattoos were lickable. And she believed him.

Imagine another relative's surprise when my child licked his arm in the buffet line at a family party. "Uncle Craig, that didn't taste very good," she whispered to him.

Since then, Uncle Craig has also encouraged her to color in his tattoos with Magic Markers. In February, she insisted we get the boxes of valentines with free tattoos to share with her nursery school classmates. There are only three other little girls in her class; I think she realized this and just wanted the other fourteen tattoos for herself.

And every time she colors with her markers, she asks, "It's okay if I get ink on myself, right Mommy?" Her hands often look like she's splashed them in a paint box. I'm convinced she's subconsciously trying to prepare me for the day she comes home with a vivid tattoo splashed across her shoulder, her ankle, or her arm. "Yes, Emma, it's alright to have ink on yourself."

There's that saying, something about how a child shall lead them. The stereotypes about tattoos are so common. The few tattoos she's seen up close might look sort of scary to a child. Yet here's my little curly-haired dynamo who thinks they're fun and pretty and wants to wear one all the time. To her, there is no incongruity between sporting a tattoo and wearing her pink plaid skirt or sleeping in her purple princess sleeping bag. She never sits as still as she does when I'm holding a wet washcloth to her arm, pressing the papered picture onto her baby smooth skin, breath bated as she waits for the magic that will transform her ordinary arms into colorful art, crowing with pride as she shows off her latest design to everyone she meets. Her enthusiasm is contagious, making a little part of me want one of my own.

Time will tell if her passion for the temporary tattoos evolves into enthusiasm for permanent ones. Maybe someday she and I will go get inked together. Until then, I've bought her a set of sparkly, tropical-themed Hello Kitty tattoos that should at least get us through the next few months. *Maybe.*

Amy Brozio-Andrews is a freelance writer and book reviewer. Her credits and clips of her work can be found on her Web site at www.amyba.com.

APPENDIX:
Frequently Asked Questions about Tattoos

Is it true that I can't go tanning with a tattoo?

It's natural to want to maintain a healthy appearance by tanning or lying out in the sun. However, those UV rays are extremely damaging to a tattoo and can quickly turn an expensive piece of art into a faded memory of what once was. You wouldn't put a Van Gogh in direct sunlight, and you shouldn't put your tattoo in it either. Use the highest SPF lotion you can find or cover yourself with clothing when you're going to be in the sun. Even short periods of sun exposure add up when you consider you will wear your tattoo for many years.

I have a family wedding coming up and don't want my relatives to see my tattoos, any suggestions?

If you're going to a wedding, family reunion, or anywhere else that you do not want your tattoo to make an appearance, you do have a few options. Products made for covering facial birthmarks and large or dark skin discoloration can also be used to cover a tattoo. There are also some products made specifically for covering tattoos, and they can be found on the Internet. It may take testing a few products to find the one that works best for your tattoo and your skin.

I have breast implants, can I still get a tattoo on my chest?

Contrary to a popular myth, breast implants cannot be punctured by the tattoo needles if someone with implants gets a tattoo on her breast. The needle does not penetrate the skin that deeply and poses no danger to the breast or to the implant. Getting implants after already having a tattoo on your breast could definitely cause a problem, however. The stretching of the skin over the implants may damage and distort the appearance of your tattoo.

Is it true that when I get pregnant the tattoo on my belly will change?

Tattoos on the belly and abdomen are very sensuous on women due to the contour and curves of the female body, but not a good idea if there is any chance of becoming pregnant. The areas of the body that stretch the most during pregnancy may damage a tattoo beyond repair. It's best to wait until your childbearing days are over so there is no chance of ruining your art.

I'm nursing my newborn, can I still get a tattoo?

When you have a baby relying on you to supply it with healthy nutrition, you don't want to risk tainting the food supply in any way. This is why it is recommended that you not get any tattoos while you are pregnant or nursing. Everything that happens to your body also happens to your unborn child, and everything that enters your body affects your milk supply. If your tattoo becomes infected or you are exposed to any kind of blood-borne illness while getting tattooed, that puts your child at a dangerous and unnecessary health risk.

Can working out at the gym affect my tattoo?

Exercise may or may not affect a new tattoo, depending on where your tattoo is and what kind of exercise you plan to do. A tattoo over a major muscle that you use during weight training may flex and contract too much and be damaging to a tattoo. Jogging with a new arm tattoo, however, probably won't make any difference. The main area of concern when it comes to exercise is sweat and dirt, which can introduce bacteria and produce infection. It's very important to shower and thoroughly—but gently—clean your tattoo immediately after you are finished working out.

I've heard getting a tattoo is extremely painful, is that true?

The pain factor is almost always the first area of concern to someone who hasn't gotten any tattoos. Unfortunately, there is no real way for anyone to tell someone else how little or how much pain they will experience. People have their own pain threshold that determines how much they can withstand. But getting a tattoo is generally not unbearable, which is why many people go back for more than one. Besides, women can usually handle a lot more pain than men, which is why we have the babies!

Will a tattoo come out okay if I have darker skin?

If you have dark skin, you may think you can't get a tattoo. Or you may think you can only get black ink and no color. This isn't necessarily true, but it has a lot to do with the level of experience of the artist. If the tattooist says she can't do it, that doesn't mean no one else can. Check around until you find someone qualified, because colored tattoos on dark skin is possible when the artist knows how to apply it.

I'm not sure I'm ready for the permanence of a tattoo but they seem so cool, any suggestions?

If you're not ready to commit to the permanence of a "real" tattoo, there are temporary alternatives. Transfer tattoos (also known as "lick and sticks") have come a long way; they are much more sophisticated and come in many designs, not just cartoon characters. Body paint or airbrushed tattoos is another temporary and fun substitute to its permanent cousin, and henna art (known as mehndi) is an ancient tradition celebrated in many cultures. Getting a permanent tattoo, if you are not completely sure or ready, is a very bad idea, so try out some of these options first.

Can my glitter body lotion affect my new tattoo?

If you have a new tattoo anywhere near where you apply powders, sprays, creams, or gels containing chemicals, be extremely careful. These products can cause irritation or even damage your tattoo. It's best to keep your tattoo temporarily covered with a towel while applying these products. Only mild, unscented lotions can be safely applied to a new tattoo.

Is it true you can't get a tattoo when you have your period?

You can physically get a tattoo when you have your period but if you have a choice, you might want to wait till it's over. When making the appointment to get your tattoo, you might want to check the calendar first and set the date for when you're not going to be in the middle of your menstrual cycle. Why? Some women experience extra tenderness and sensitivity during this time, making the process of getting a tattoo more painful. If you're concerned about pain, you might want to plan your tattoo appointments around your period schedule.

Will losing or gaining weight really affect my tattoo?

Women tend to fluctuate in their weight more than men, which means their tattoos endure a lot more abuse. The good news is that tattoos, just like our skin, are very forgiving and can stretch and contract through many weight ups and downs. Significant weight changes that happen over a short period of time, however, may be too much for your tattoo. If the skin sags or stretches unevenly, the tattoo may become distorted.

I have some stretch marks from my pregnancy, will they affect me getting a tattoo?

Stretch marks cause our skin enough problems, but they can cause even more issues for a tattoo. Deep or dark stretch marks resulting from fast weight gain can render a tattoo irreparable. However, stretch marks can sometimes be tattooed over or around to make them less evident. Small, thin, and light stretch marks can usually be tattooed over quite easily. Large, deep, or dark stretch marks may not be tattooable, but they could possibly be incorporated into a design to make them more attractive.

Is it possible to be allergic to the ink used in tattoos?

Although it is not common, allergic reactions to tattoo ink do happen. Particularly shades of red and green tend to contain ingredients that may cause a reaction in more sensitive clients. A mild reaction could result in an itchy rash, swelling, or oozing. A severe reaction could result in anaphylaxis. If you are prone to allergies, have a sensitive constitution, or a lowered immune system, a tattoo may not be a wise choice.

I love the feet tattoos that are becoming so popular now, what can you tell me about them?

Women, especially, appreciate the subtle beauty of a foot tattoo. They are also the best candidates for such a tattoo, since they're generally not as abusive to their feet as men are. But we still wear socks and shoes or get tanned on our bare feet when we're out in the sun, all of which can be very detrimental to a tattoo. Socks rub and hold in sweat. Shoes rub and suffocate our feet. The sun is damaging to tattoo ink. Caring for a new foot tattoo is very demanding and shouldn't be taken lightly.

I'm nervous about getting a tattoo, would it be okay to have a few drinks beforehand to loosen me up?

You may be nervous about getting a tattoo, but having a drink isn't going to make things easier on you. Alcohol thins the blood, making you bleed more readily while you're being tattooed. That makes things much more difficult for your artist and can cause more scabbing after the fact. Also, no professional artist will tattoo you if you're drunk or your ability to make decisions has been impaired in any way.

I'm on a prescription medication for an issue unrelated to my skin, do I have to let the tattoo artist know?

If you take any kind of prescription medication, it's important that you disclose that information to your artist before getting tattooed. It could indicate that you have a condition that would make tattooing you dangerous, and the tattooist may recommend you not get one. But also, certain medications have been known to induce the body to reject the ink as foreign matter and flush it out into the bloodstream.

I have some moles on my back that I hate, so I'd like to hide them with a tattoo, can the artist tattoo over the moles?

You may be embarrassed if you have a mole or skin growth and want to know if you can cover it up with a tattoo. This is not advisable because moles and skin growths are your body's first warning signal if there is cancer in the cells. Having them tattooed over would make it difficult for you to detect subtle changes in size or color that could indicate a problem and could ultimately save your life. It's best to leave them alone.

I worry about my boss's reaction if I get a tattoo, do you think it's still looked down upon in the business world?

Depending on the career field you are in or hoping to enter, tattoos may get in your way. Unethical as it may be, many employers still discriminate against people—especially women—with tattoos. You can still get tattoos, but you'll need to be sure that they are in locations on your body that are easily covered up with your particular uniform, whatever that may be. Visible tattoos raise a big red flag with potential employers and can seriously hurt your career or advancement goals.

WORKS REFERENCED

Amy Krakow, *The Total Tattoo Book* (New York: Warner Books, Inc., 1994)

Margot Mifflin, *Bodies of Subversion: A Secret History of Women and Tattoo*, 2nd edition (New York: Juno Books, 2001)

"Bettie Page Bio," Betty Page Official Web site, *www.bettiepage.com/about/bio.html*

"Juli Moon Bio," Juli Moon Designs Web site, *www.julimoon.com/main.html*

"Kari Barba Bio," Outer Limits, Anaheim Web site, *www.outerlimitstattoo.com/anaheim.html*

"Mick Michieli-Beasley Bio," Dragon Moon Studio Web site, *www.dragon-moon.com/artists/bio_mick.htm*

"Pat Fish Bio," Lucky Fish Web site, *www.luckyfish.com*

"Pat Sinatra Bio," Pat's Tats Web site, *www.patstats.com/pat/patbio.html*

"SuzAnne Fauser Tribute," Rusty Savage's Studio Tattoo Web site, *www.studiotattoo.com/suzanne.html*

"Tattoo History from A to Z," Tattoo Archive Web site, *www .tattooarchive.com/tattoo_history.htm*

"Tattooed Ladies Defined Outer Boundaries of Changing Society," Research Profile Web site, *www.uwm.edu/Dept/ Grad_Sch/Publications/ResearchProfile/issues/vol-27-no-01/ synopsis3.html*

"Tattooing the Beehive," *SLUG Magazine* Web site, *www.slugmag .com/modules.php?op=modload&name=News&file=article& sid=205&mode=thread*

ABOUT THE EDITOR

Karen Hudson is a wife, mother, author, educator, and body art enthusiast. Since her first exposure to the modern world of tattoos, Karen decided that she wanted to devote herself heart and soul to the continuation of this ancient art form. She began her education at the very studio where she received her first tattoo. A year later she found her calling—an opportunity to educate those looking for solid, unbiased information. As the About .com Guide to Tattoos and Body Piercings, she has continued to build on what she started—coaching, educating, and encouraging those who are looking for a safe way to express themselves through body modification.